DEFENSE AGAINST FAMINE

The *Chemistry in Action Series* has been designed to give the interested layman a thorough introduction to the many different sides of the chemical industry. Prepared under the joint supervision of the Educational Activities Committee of the Manufacturing Chemists' Association and Doubleday & Company, Inc., each volume focuses on a particular segment of the chemical industry and relates the pure chemical science to the final products met in everyday life. The volumes have each been written by distinguished authorities in the field.

AUTHOR BIOGRAPHY

A. V. Slack is Chief of the Applied Science Branch, Division of Chemical Development for the Tennessee Valley Authority. He has been deeply involved in the field of fertilizer research and development since his graduation from the University of Tennessee, progressing from work at the bench to head of applied research. Dr. Slack has traveled throughout the world investigating trends in fertilizer development and use in both advanced and underdeveloped countries.

DEFENSE AGAINST FAMINE

The Role of the Fertilizer Industry

A. V. SLACK

PREPARED UNDER THE SPONSORSHIP OF
THE MANUFACTURING CHEMISTS' ASSOCIATION

Garden City, New York
DOUBLEDAY & COMPANY, INC.
1970

Library of Congress Catalog Card Number 76–104982
Copyright © 1970 by A. V. Slack
All Rights Reserved
Printed in the United States of America
First Edition

Contents

DEFENSE AGAINST FAMINE

Chapter 1

Food for the World's People

Each living thing must draw on its environment for materials to sustain existence. There must be oxygen for the combustion processes that maintain body temperature and energy of men and animals, carbon dioxide for photosynthesis by vegetable species, and water to maintain and replenish body fluids of all living matter. In addition, various substances, generally called foods, must be supplied to both plants and animals to serve as raw materials for the many chemical reactions that constitute the life processes. When the supply of these materials is cut off, the organism may live for some time by using food stored within its own tissues, but as this becomes exhausted the time comes when some key chemical reaction can no longer take place, and death occurs.

To early man, the search for food was the most important phase of his existence. He could hide in caves to avoid the predatory animals that looked on him as prey, and the cave also protected him from the rigors of the climate, with which he had not yet learned to cope. But the daily need for food drove him forth to hunt for animals that were weak enough and slow enough for him to catch, and for plants that experience had taught him he could digest. Thus like all wild things he was forced to expose himself to the hazards of his environment in the ceaseless search for the chemical compounds his body needed. Air and water were easy to come by, but food was not.

The Beginning of Agriculture

It would be most interesting to be able to follow the long course of man's battle with his environment, culminating in the relative mastery that he has today. But early man was a poor historian so we can only guess about the things that happened—events of individual discovery or innovation that probably were little noted at the time but which in retrospect become major steps forward in the rise of man. There were, of course, the notable discoveries of how to kindle and maintain a fire, how to put to use the fortunate geometry of the circle in making a wheel, how to make metal for tools, and how to set down his thoughts in a permanent record. But somewhere along the way, an event took place that was at least as important as these, and possibly more so. Some ancient genius made a correlation between the fall of seeds from a mature plant and the sprouting of similar plants at that spot the following spring. Perhaps he went further and conceived the idea that he could gather the seed and plant it in a place of his own choosing, or perhaps, as is more likely, the knowledge of how new plants are formed was passed on from father to son until in some distant generation the great step to planned planting of seed was made. This may have been man's very first adventure into constructive control of his environment; after centuries of accepting things as they were he moved into an era in which valuable plants were propagated and nurtured and undesirable plants were destroyed, thus changing the normal balance in nature.

When the first seed was planted purposely, agriculture was born. The tempo of innovation then picked up, requiring perhaps only a few generations to go, say, from scattering of seeds to planting in rows, or from letting the plant fend for itself to removing weeds and cultivating the soil. Agriculture became a major steppingstone for the further progress of man, because with planned production of food he could supply his needs in something less than his total waking hours and hence had time for other pursuits and other innovations.

The change from gathering seeds and fruit where they grew naturally to planting seed where the plants could be protected and nurtured probably took place about 7000 or 8000 B.C. No one knows where this practice began, but the early traces of agriculture in the valley of the Nile and the river valleys eastward in Asia indicate that it was in this part of the world man first made the shift from hunter to farmer—a prerequisite to civilization and progress. The soils of these areas were well suited to growing of crops and produced abundantly, so much so that in one growing season enough food for the entire year could be produced. With this unaccustomed leisure, Neolithic man no doubt wasted his time at first, but eventually the more inventive and industrious made the other great discoveries of prehistory. The finding that certain rocks could be heated with wood or charcoal to give copper and iron—and that these metals were useful in making tools and weapons—was the first real beginning of manufacturing, far advanced over the crude fashioning of stone and wood of earlier centuries. Trade began, and with it the commercial exchange that allowed one man to be a metalsmith and another a farmer growing enough food for both. Cities were built, where these exchanges could be made more conveniently. Governments were set up, small and informal at first but rapidly developing into forces that controlled the lives of Bronze and Iron Age peoples. And the art of organized war was developed, bringing with it excursions by one despot into the territory of another or into the lands of those not yet blessed with government. This, plus the travels of traders, began the processes of colonization and shifting of populations that gradually spread the early civilization over Asia and Europe.

Agriculture had become the accepted method for producing food but progress in improving farming methods was very slow, not nearly comparable with the rapid development of metal working and other types of manufacture. A few crude farming tools were developed and animals were put to the task of plowing the soil. Beyond this, changes in farming came slowly over many centuries.

Early man probably gave little thought to why plants grew when he planted seeds, and what factors might make them grow better or worse. Trees grew, and weeds grew, so cultivated plants naturally must grow. There was little reason for him to consider the differences in the situations, that trees and weeds die and go back into the soil but cultivated plants are harvested and removed from the place where they grew. He did not know that returning dead plants to the soil returns also the nutrient elements that plants take up from the soil during their growth and fruiting, and that interfering with this natural cycle gradually depletes the soil of the materials essential for plant nutrition.

This phenomenon would not have been noticed by the early farmers of the great river basins anyway, for the fertility of their soils was kept at a high level by the river itself. Each year, for example, the Nile rose obligingly from its banks, during the season when no crops were growing, and deposited over the farmlands a layer of rich topsoil looted from the high country far to the unknown South. The river valley farmers accepted this as evidence of a supernatural generosity and indeed made the Nile one of their gods to show their gratitude.

In other places, where there were no rivers to constantly replenish the nutrient resources of the soil, the early farmers soon found that after a long period of tilling a particular plot of land, the yields began to decrease. To most of them this also was not any great problem, for there was plenty of land and not many people. When the soil no longer produced the needed food, it was easy to move on and break again the virgin sod. To many this was a normal thing, for they lived a nomadic life, depending mainly on raising animals to supply food and clothing. The growing of forage crops for feeding animals had not yet developed, so they lived in tents and moved from place to place where grass and wild grain could be found. The farming they did was incidental, and they were never in one place long enough to exhaust the soil.

Others were not so fortunate as the nomads, who ranged over the open country and could start a new farming operation merely by digging and planting. In the forest country of eastern Europe, moving to new land required removing the mass of growing and dead brush and trees that covered the soil. There is evidence that early man developed there the technique of burning off "new ground," a practice that was still popular among the farmers who drove west across North America in the pioneer days.

Gradually the situation changed. As populations increased and governments grew stronger, the growing importance of property rights made it more and more difficult for farmers to find new land when the old was exhausted. Man then came face to face with a problem that has plagued him ever since, that of soil conservation. Regardless of what happens to natural resources such as forests, mineral deposits, or scenic beauty, it is essential that the upper eight inches of the earth's surface be kept in a condition approaching that in which man found it. This is a many-pronged problem, including not only maintenance of the quantity and quality of the mineral content, the subject of this book, but also the physical structure of the soil and in some instances the very presence of the soil, since poor farming practice can produce disastrous erosion.

We should not gather from the foregoing that the nutrient elements in the soil always become depleted rapidly as farming continues. The situation varies, depending on sequence of crop types (plants differ in their appetite for particular nutrients), intensity of cultivation, and incidental fertilization. In an extreme case, in which the same crop is grown repeatedly and nothing, not even plant residue, is returned to the soil, productivity can drop to a very low level in a generation. But such an extreme fortunately is rare. The usual situation is that productivity gradually declines, on a curve approaching a minimum level that ordinarily can be maintained without changing the farming practice.

We should also be careful to avoid the conclusion that maintaining the nutrient content of soil is the only requirement for optimum crop growth. There are many requisites, each of them a subject of concern and of intense continuing study by many research people. The soil must be protected from erosion, there must be organic material present, a proper soil physical structure is essential, soil acidity must be adjusted, plant type must be correlated with growing situation, and the growing plant must be protected from its natural enemies—drought, disease, weeds, and insects. All this makes agriculture a very complex subject. We shall restrict ourselves in this book to fertilization, which, as the name implies, is the technology of maintaining the fertility of the soil.

Early Fertilization

Like most of the great lessons that man has had to learn, knowledge of plant nutrition came slowly and with great difficulty. Early recognition that the land could lose its fertility was followed by a long period of accepting the fact but not doing anything about it—other than accepting a meager yield from starved plants or moving on to new and more fertile ground. We do not know the circumstances of the first recognition that plants need food as much as animals and people do. But someone noted that when certain materials happened to find their way to the soil, then plants grew better at that spot. Very likely the droppings from animals as they grazed brought about the first such recognition. Even today it is easy to note in pastures the spots where droppings have made the grass greener and higher. Or perhaps the skeletons of animals as they lay on the ground, with the grass growing high and strong through the rib cage, brought to some ancient the realization that natural materials returned to the soil brings to it new life. Or again, nomadic tribes returning to old grazing places may have noted the lush grass growing in the ashes of last year's campfires.

Whatever the beginning, early man learned to apply manure, bones, and ashes to the soil. And indeed for centuries these were the fertilizers on which farmers depended to maintain soil fertility. Those who burned forests to clear new land for farming soon learned that the burning had a great advantage beyond making the soil accessible; the ashes made the soil so fertile that unusually large, or bumper, crops could be grown—until the nutrients were exhausted and it was time to move on, or, as later farmers realized, to apply more nutrient to the soil. It was not understood then, of course, but we know today that burning the forests released from the wood in a few moments mineral nutrients that would have taken years for release in the normal course of decay.

Although not realized by early peoples, the use of manure, bones, and ashes was a substitute for the natural method of maintaining soil fertility—return of all the minerals in the plant to the soil by the fall and decay of vegetation at the spot where it grew. The same is accomplished by returning the droppings and bones of animals that eat the plant—since this returns all the minerals consumed by the animal—and the ashes of plant residues that animals do not eat.

The earliest recordings of history contain many references to natural materials as fertilizers. The value of manure is mentioned in mythology as early as 900 to 700 B.C.; in the Greek epic poem, *The Odyssey,* supposedly written by Homer in that period, the manuring of vineyards by the father of Odysseus is mentioned, and it is said that Argos, the faithful hound of Odysseus, was lying on a manure pile when his master returned after twenty years. Later, between 450 and 350 B.C., Xenophon made a direct recommendation for manuring, saying that "there is nothing so good as manure." His advice was heeded, for it is recorded that truck gardens and olive groves around ancient Athens were fertilized by city sewage carried in canals.

The fertilizing value of dead bodies and bones is also recognized in early writings, by Archilochus as early as 700 B.C. In the Bible, in Deuteronomy, the people were told to pour the blood of animals on the ground. Some centuries later Omar Khayyám stated it poetically:

> I sometimes think that
> never grows so red
> The Rose as where some
> buried Caesar bled.

The Bible also records early practice in burning undesirable plant growth to fertilize the soil, and use of ashes is referred to frequently in Greek and Roman literature. Cato, for example, recommended that prunings in vineyards be burned and the ashes plowed into the soil.

Other important discoveries were made in these middle centuries. Although most of the emphasis was on returning to the soil the substance of the original plant, there was the beginning of the important concept that nutrients can be taken from other sources, perhaps some distance away, and brought to the soil. This was a significant advancement because it was a necessary antecedent to the later development of the fertilizer industry.

Both Theophrastus and Pliny, early Greek and Roman writers, mentioned the use of saltpeter—naturally occurring potassium nitrate—as a fertilizer. Such use is also mentioned in the Bible, in the book of Luke. As surface deposits of saltpeter could be found in dry areas such as the Middle East, the material was available to early farmers. But the discovery that it could be removed, carried to a farm, and there used profitably to increase crop production required more imagination on the part of the discoverer than did the earlier recognitions of the value of ashes and animal remains. The development was particularly noteworthy because it was the first departure from organic sources of plant nutrients. As we shall see later, the fertilizer industry of today could never have developed without a shift to inorganic sources.

Another advancement was learning that calcareous, alkaline materials such as marl (clay mixed with calcium carbonate) could be dug from natural deposits and used to improve soil productivity. Early farmers probably classed this as a fertilizer along with other natural materials, but today we know that the marl helped not by supplying plant nutrients but by correcting an acid condition of the soil. This was another lesson man had to learn: the natural tendency of most soils in the natural state is to reach a level of acidity that many plants—of the type that we like as food—cannot tolerate very well.

Sometime during early agriculture another advancement occurred, this one of unique importance because it involved a chemical reaction that converted an element from an unavailable state to a form usable by plants. This was not a chemical operation planned by anyone, which was too great a step forward at that time, but rather a recognition that a naturally occurring phenomenon could be put to use in improving soil fertility. It was found that when certain plants were grown, then other and different plants grew better at that location later. Virgil (70–19 B.C.) wrote that ". . . you will sow there yellow wheat, whence before you have taken up the joyful pulse, with rustling pods, or the vetch's slender offspring and the bitter lupine's brittle stalks, and rustling grove." Today we know the pulse, vetch, and lupine as legumes, plants that have the ability, in conjunction with microorganisms that live on their roots, of taking inert nitrogen from the air and converting it to a form that plants can use. When the legume dies, the nitrogen compounds remain for use by succeeding generations of plants, even of different variety.

The growing of legumes as a means of fertilizing the soil was the first instance, although unrecognized at the time as such, of taking an inert substance from its natural state and converting it to a useful fertilizer material. These words could be used today as a definition of the fertilizer industry.

The step forward in recognizing the value of legumes required an advanced degree of data correlation for the time; perhaps it was done by the Greeks, who in the period 800 to 200 B.C. extended the frontiers of knowledge at a rate far greater than in preceding eras, or for that matter, for centuries to come. The learned men of the day had inquiring minds, and the Greek philosophers still have an important place in the realm of human thought. It is unfortunate that their thinking did not evolve the experimental approach. If it had, then there might have been enough progress to avoid the blight of the ensuing Dark Ages, in which not only was there a slowing of development but even a suppression of original thought.

The Romans who came after the Greeks copied their culture and technological departures, particularly in agriculture. From the combined cultures there developed a considerable insight into the factors that affect plant growth. Many of the practices recommended were good ones and are still followed today; others reflected a misunderstanding of the basic mechanisms involved, and it was over fifteen centuries before planned experimentation aimed at unravelling these mysteries began.

After the fall of the Roman Empire, progress in agricultural development slowed to almost a standstill. Even writings on the subject, prevalent in the Greek and Roman eras, no longer appeared; it was not until the thirteenth century, when Pietro Crescenzi (1230–1307) wrote a history of agricultural practices, that anything significant was published. Then ensued another barren period, until the seventeenth century finally gave birth to the experimental method as a way of developing understanding of natural phenomena.

Birth of the Fertilizer Industry

The intellectual awakening that began in the seventeenth century brought the attention of many thinkers and investigators to the problems of plant nutrition. Numerous theories were advanced, many of them quite erroneous, but gradually a science of plant nutrition developed. The principles of plant feeding will be set forth in the next chapter; it will suffice here to say that three chemical elements—nitrogen, phosphorus, and potassium—became recognized as the major ones needed by plants, and that the natural materials used from antiquity were effective because they supplied these elements. Manure contains nitrogen in a usable form, phosphorus is a major constituent of bones, and ashes are rich in potassium.

With the better understanding of plant growth came the first stirrings of a fertilizer industry, but it was not until about the middle of the nineteenth century, less than a hundred years ago, that knowledge was advanced enough to serve as a sound basis for the new technology. At this point, we might ask why a new technology was needed: if the plant substance was being returned to the soil as manure (animal and human), animal remains, and plant residues, why was anything further needed? The answer is that as the world became more crowded and other technologies brought in their complicating effects, it became more and more difficult to return plant products to the soil. Meat animals were shipped to slaughterhouses far from where they grew; human excreta, a disagreeable material never popular as a fertilizer in Europe anyway, became less available as cities developed sewage systems; and plant residues, particularly in the form of household garbage, became more remote from their origin as the practice of shipping grains and vegetables long distances developed. Such natural materials have relatively low concentrations of plant nutrients, and therefore they are seldom economical if they must be transported very far to the farm. In the earlier and simpler economy, when most people lived on farms, return of nutrients was fairly simple, and this is still the practice in the less developed areas of the world. The industrialized nations, in contrast, cannot afford the labor required in handling and shipping low-grade materials.

Another important finding in the beginning of the present era was that nature can be improved upon. The level of fertility found in virgin soil is not necessarily the maximum that can be attained or the most economical to maintain. When large amounts of plant nutrients are applied, and other advanced farming practices followed, the land can be made to yield far more than it could in its original state when it was first broken to the plow. Hence the cycling of plant nutrients can be improved upon by bringing in nutrients from other sources. As will be discussed later, this is a factor of great world importance today.

For these reasons man turned to manufacture of fertilizers as a replacement for the old practice of using natural materials. This required a shift to inorganic substances, for organic compounds of nitrogen, phosphorus, and potassium are too difficult and expensive to synthesize. It had already been learned in prehistory—in the Bronze and Iron Ages—that many of the elements needed by man have been conveniently concentrated during past eons at certain spots in the earth's crust; from such deposits came the iron and copper used by prehistoric man and from them come the metals used today. The same was true for phosphorus and potassium; ores were discovered that could be mined and processed at far less cost than for collecting and handling waste materials from plants. Nitrogen presented a different problem, of which more will be said later.

The new industry started very slowly. Phosphorus received first attention, probably because the early experimenters found that bones did not stimulate plant growth as rapidly as manure and ashes. We know today that the calcium phosphate in bones does not dissolve very fast in the soil, whereas the nitrogen and potassium compounds in manure and ashes are readily soluble. In 1831, bones were first treated with sulfuric acid to make them more soluble and a better fertilizer. Not long afterward phosphate ore was substituted for bone and the fertilizer industry was on its way.

The new technology had its critics. Many of those accustomed to the natural, organic fertilizers were quite dubious about the efficacy of the new materials, not withstanding the fact that saltpeter (potassium nitrate) is an inorganic ore that for centuries had been used with good results. The terms "artificial" and "chemical" were applied to the new fertilizers, often disparagingly. Today we realize that everything is "chemical" and that use of the term to distinguish between manufactured and naturally produced materials is not justified. Neither is the term "artificial" very helpful, since it matters little whether a chemical reaction is carried out in a manufacturing plant or in a natural growth process. The product is the same, except that nature does not usually achieve as high a degree of purity. Nevertheless, criticism of manufactured fertilizers has continued up to the present day. The resistance has decreased, however, in the face of the obvious accomplishments of "chemical" fertilizers; today the criticism seems to be mainly by writers and publishers who can be suspected of profiting by their eloquent exposition of the merits of "organic" fertilizer.

It should not be concluded from the foregoing that there was a sudden shift from natural materials to manufactured fertilizer. There were many natural byproducts that were economically recovered and used as fertilizer even with the new manufacturing processes available; some of these are still recovered today—slaughterhouse wastes, for example—but the amount is only a minute percentage of the total fertilizer produced. In the latter half of the nineteenth century and the early part of the twentieth, however, such materials made up a major part of fertilizer consumption. As a result, the industry gained the reputation of being a scavenger operation—and an odorous one as well because of the manures and the animal and fish processing wastes involved. Even today many people unfamiliar with the industry seem to think that odor is a sign of quality in fertilizer. Perhaps this is why many people who work in the field prefer the terms "plant food" or "plant nutrient." Byproducts now are a minor factor, however, and the growing stature of the industry is rapidly dispelling the misconceptions of the past.

After treatment of phosphate ore with acid began (the product was called superphosphate), phosphate manufacture grew fairly rapidly but there was still little activity in nitrogen and potassium processing methods. New ores were discovered, however, that contained these elements in a form available to plants without further processing. One of these, potassium chloride, replaced potassium nitrate almost completely, which is important because potassium nitrate deposits are few and small. The chloride, in contrast, is probably closer to being an inexhaustible resource than any other mineral used by man. It is the current major potash source and should be for centuries to come.

The main replacement for manures as a source of nitrogen in this period was sodium nitrate, a large natural deposit of which had been discovered in a desert valley in Chile in 1809. Mining and shipping began around the middle of that century and the product soon became a major world supplier of fertilizer nitrogen; its use receded only when the great developments of the twentieth century brought on more economical nitrogen materials.

Late in the eighteenth century a discourse was published that showed how rapidly concepts of plant nutrient supply had advanced and matured. Thomas Malthus, an English clergyman who gave considerable thought to world problems, became concerned over the food supply for the growing populations. With remarkable insight, he foresaw the population explosion of the twentieth century and the problems it might bring in growing enough food on the limited amount of farm land available. He recognized the value of fertilizer in increasing the food supply but considered that not enough could be supplied to avert famine and, as a consequence, major political disorders.

The main question that made Malthus' gloomy prediction a serious possibility was the supply of fertilizer nitrogen. Manures and legumes were only a partial answer, not equal to the great need Malthus foresaw. The discovery of sodium nitrate in Chile was a fortunate circumstance, but the deposit was an isolated, limited one, obviously inadequate for the future world demand.

Malthus' forebodings were remembered in 1914–18, when German submarines cut off the United States from the Chilean deposits; fortunately, the war did not last long enough to cause any great difficulty, and it was in about the same period that the Germans themselves solved the problem, at least for many decades to come. In 1914, Fritz Haber, Karl Bosch and coworkers developed a method for converting inert atmospheric nitrogen into ammonia, a compound of hydrogen and nitrogen that can supply nitrogen to plants and is economical to produce. The main raw materials for ammonia production are oil, natural gas, or coal, so that Haber's process shifted the nitrogen supply, in effect, from a relatively small deposit, in a remote part of the world, to the great fossil fuel reserves that are widely available over the earth's surface. This development, one of the great historical discoveries in applied chemistry, was a major milestone in fertilizer technology.

After the development of ammonia synthesis, fertilizer development accelerated at a rapid pace. The advances, too numerous to even mention in this introductory chapter, included ever higher nutrient concentration, better physical properties, progress on problems of chemical decomposition before use, new physical forms, and more economical methods of production. Beginning about 1950, the pace accelerated again; the slope of the fertilizer consumption curve increased sharply and major chemical producers who had never made fertilizers before began to move into this promising field.

Today fertilizer production is a major segment of the world chemical industry. Production capacity is increasing at a fantastic rate, with new plants being announced almost daily in all corners of the world. The production technology of even fifteen years ago is well on the way to being obsolete. The new technology, which will be the subject of several of the succeeding chapters, has brought new economy and a greater potential for food production. Byproduct materials, particularly of the organic type, no longer are important; the major materials of today are phosphate and potash ores, sulfur (for sulfuric acid), and the fossil fuels.

The Modern Dilemma

In the past we have had many disciplines or fields of specialization taking part in the basic sciences of plant growth and nutrition and the applied science of food production. Chemists provide data for new fertilizer processes, chemical and other engineers develop and prove them, economists evaluate the use of fertilizer as a farming practice, agronomists consider the variables in plant nutrition, soil scientists concern themselves with the nature of the soil and its suitability for plant growth, and many disciplines are involved in study of how to protect the growing plant against its natural enemies.

In the early 1960s, another voice has been added to the chorus—that of the demographer, who studies the trends in population growth and their effect on world affairs. Like Malthus, the demographers of today predict a future in which food production will be a critical and all-important problem. Indeed, the warnings we hear are almost an echo of those by Malthus over 150 years ago—and which might have come to point earlier but for the interjection of ammonia synthesis early in this century.

The situation is stark and dreadful in its simplicity. The population of the world doubled in the period 1600 to 1830, doubled again by 1920, and now has doubled again in less than fifty years. By A.D. 2000 there may be well over 6,000,000,000 people to feed, but from a usable land area that has decreased rather than increased over the history of agriculture. Only about 3.5 percent of the earth's surface (3,850,000,000 acres) is presently suitable for crop production. Even if marginal land, such as shallow areas on ocean shores, were reclaimed and developed, only about 5,500,000,000 acres—5 percent of the total world area—would be available.

Feeding the world with less than an acre available per person is a gloomy prospect. And this is only part of the problem, because the highest rates of population growth are in the countries least able to afford them—countries in which poor farming practices restrict yields to levels much below those in the more advanced nations. For example, the population growth rate per year in Latin America is about 2.9 percent, a rate that in a generation will double the number of people to be fed. In contrast, the rate of increase in developed areas such as Europe and Japan is only 0.9 percent.

There are obvious steps that need to be taken—education of the great mass of illiterates, implementation of birth control methods, and a raising of the economic level, which almost always decreases birth rate. But these are relatively slow methods. It is highly unlikely that they can be put into effect fast enough to prevent major malnutrition and starvation in problem areas such as Latin America.

The consensus is that increased crop production is the only immediate solution, even though a stop gap one. This also involves several tools—better seed varieties, pest and disease control, better tillage practice, greater fertilizer use—but again many of these probably cannot be pushed fast enough to have major immediate impact. There seems to be general agreement that massive production of fertilizer, and some means to ensure its use, will give the maximum thrust to food production in the shortest time.

Here then is the dilemma of modern man. He has gone far since his cave-dwelling days, where we met him at the beginning of this chapter. No longer does he fear his environment, but has conquered it and made it the basis of an attainable standard of living undreamed of even a half century ago. The gathering of food, once the activity that filled his days, now requires, in the advanced sections of his society, only minor attention. But all this is threatened by his inability to control his own numbers, to keep the number of people in line with the number of acres on which food can be grown.

There is no simple answer to this problem. It could be said that the advanced peoples might continue to enjoy their present abundance of food, which, with further agricultural development expected, is not threatened very much by the current modest rate of population growth, while the problem areas solved their problem by starvation. Even if this were acceptable from the humanitarian standpoint, it might not be politically. Hunger is a prime source of political unrest that involves the well-fed nations even when they attempt to stand aloof.

Fertilizer technology thus has assumed an importance that it never had before. It is not the only answer to the world's problems, of which there are many other than hunger. But in the next quarter century it may be found the most effective tool for staving off the consequences of one major problem that so far man has not been able to solve.

He may yet solve it if he can buy the time.

CHAPTER 2

Background for Plant Nutrition

Early in the sixteenth century, in the general period marked by the voyages of the great explorers and the consequent widening knowledge of world geography, there were the stirrings of another type of exploration—into the unknown areas beyond the limited early knowledge of natural processes and the nature of the many phases of man's environment. For some 25 centuries men had sought for truth (with a very few notable exceptions) merely by thinking about it—much as if the explorers had sat at home and reasoned out the location and nature of distant lands. The alchemists in particular looked for the philosopher's stone and the elixir of life but did their searching mainly from their armchairs and depended on a mixture of mysticism, superstition, tradition, and theology. As sometimes happens today, they were more enamored with the method than the objective, and therefore accomplished nothing.

Philippus Paracelsus (1493–1541), a brilliant but drunken Swiss, promoted the radical view that chemists should set their goals more in line with their abilities and aim at things less ambitious than changing base metal to gold. This was an example of a new type of thinking that gradually spread across Europe, in which opinion was excluded and experimental data raised to a level of esteem that it had not reached before. Thus the scientific method entered into a new era of acceptance and a rapid expansion in man's understanding of nature began.

The Early Investigators

One of the first fields subjected to the new method of study was agriculture. Among the early researchers was

Sir Francis Bacon, who made many simple observations of growing plants and advanced explanations; practically all were wrong but a good start had been made.

At that time chemistry was still a largely unexplored science. Following the logic of Aristotle, men considered water to be one of the basic elements and the one out of which plants were formed. Jan Baptista van Helmont, a Belgian chemist who subscribed to this view, carried out a most interesting experiment that proved to him the correctness of the hypothesis but really proved only that the experimental method is a tricky thing, of value only when used with great caution. He put a weighed amount of soil in a vessel, set in it a willow shoot of known weight, and waited five years. Then he weighed the willow and found that it had gained 164 pounds. The soil still weighed the same; it had been covered to exclude dust so the only material added to the system was the water—rain or distilled water—that van Helmont had applied. Thus the obvious conclusion was that the plant growth came only from the water, by some mysterious transmutation. This carefully conducted experiment, a fine example of the new scientific method, had led directly to an answer as erroneous as any the alchemists had ever reached.

Van Helmont had failed to meet one of the main requisites of the scientific approach: all possibilities of error must be carefully considered and eliminated experimentally before a conclusion is attempted. It did not occur to him that the willow could absorb something from the atmosphere. More than a century elapsed before it was recognized that carbon dioxide from the air is essential to plant growth and supplies most of the weight of the plant.

The phenomenon of photosynthesis—by which carbon dioxide is absorbed and becomes part of the plant substance—is not directly a part of the fertilizer story, but we should consider it here to make the account complete.

The reaction of carbon dioxide and water in living plants (photosynthesis) is an absolute essential to the existence of man. A highly simplified version is: $(6x)CO_2 + (5x) H_2O \longrightarrow (C_6H_{10}O_5)_x + (6x)O_2$. The $(C_6H_{10}O_5)_x$ is cellulose, one of the main constituents of many plants and a major food for animals, which in turn become food for man; many other carbonaceous materials—carbohydrates, fats, proteins—are produced in plants by similar reactions and make up another important part of our food supply.

To the chemist these reactions are remarkable because they run backward, from a lower level of energy to a higher one, which is contrary to the laws of thermodynamics. We would ordinarily expect cellulose and oxygen to react with vigor and form carbon dioxide and water, which is what happens when wood burns. When we sit by the fire on a winter night we are observing a complete reversal of the

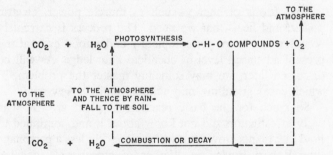

Fig. 1 The carbon cycle, a very important natural process, takes carbon dioxide from the air and water from the soil and combines them through the medium of photosynthesis to carbon-hydrogen-oxygen compounds and to free oxygen that is released to the atmosphere. In turn, oxygen from the atmosphere reacts with these compounds and converts them back to atmospheric carbon dioxide and water vapor.

reaction that took place in past summers when the tree that produced the firewood was growing. The fire completes the natural cycle shown in Figure 1.

The "uphill" reaction of carbon dioxide and water is due to a very complex substance called chlorophyll, present in plant leaves and possessing the ability to absorb energy from sunlight. The energy thus brought in raises the total energy of the system and pushes it to formation of the high-energy compounds formed and stored in the growing plant. These compounds then return to lower energy levels by three courses; they may be (1) consumed by men and animals to supply energy by reaction with oxygen in low-temperature combustion processes within the body, (2) burned with oxygen in high-temperature combustion to supply heat or power, or (3) if unused as food or fuel, subjected to natural decay by very slow reaction with oxygen.

In effect, photosynthesis by means of chlorophyll converts light energy, which has too low an intensity for practical use, to a level high enough for supplying the various forms of energy—such as muscle power, electric power, and heat—that we need. The process is extremely complex and is not yet completely understood even at the present advanced level of chemical knowledge. As will be discussed later, we may someday master the problem, in which case agriculture may take an entirely new turn.

So much for the basic reaction in plant growth. The early investigators did not know about it and continued to hold that plants grow from water alone. No less a personage than Robert Boyle, the "father of chemistry," repeated van Helmont's experiment and reached the same conclusion. He went farther and argued that worms and insects are produced from decay of plants and therefore also come from transmutation of water. The difficulty with these findings, which now seem ludicrous, was not so much the error itself but the fact that they took attention away from the soil as a factor in plant growth. If water were the only raw material needed, then the only function of the soil was to serve as a mechanical support for the plant and as a water reservoir. Until research was centered on the soil the science of plant nutrition could not be developed.

There followed a period of groping in which little progress was made in reconciling the water transmutation theory with the well-known fact that certain materials added to the soil promote plant growth. The water theory was finally laid to rest at about the beginning of the eighteenth century by John Woodward, who grew mint in distilled water, Hyde Park sewer water, and Hyde Park water that had been shaken with earth. The mint grew much larger with the Hyde Park water and even better with the water-soil extract. He also measured the amount of water taken up and found that the weight of water per unit of plant weight gain was not the same for the different types of water. Woodward's conclusion was that the plant takes up something besides water. He was wrong in his further conclusions, however, for he considered that the unknown material taken up came from the earth; in his words: ". . . a great part of the terrestrial matter, mixt with the water, passes up into the plant along with it, and . . . the plant is more or less augmented in proportion as the water contains a greater or less quantity of that matter, from all of which we may reasonably infer, that Earth, and not Water, is the matter that constitutes vegetation."

(It is worthy of note that Woodward's report appeared in a journal called *Philosophical Transactions* in 1699. Today it would not occur to us to publish experimental work in a philosophical journal but in his day science had not yet developed and presumably there was no other place to publish it.)

The confusion continued. A few statements taken from

the writings of the era show the difficulties early investigators had without a science to guide them:

> Air could be no part of it (*the tree*) because air has
> no greater specific gravity than the incumbent atmosphere
> and could not be of any weight in it.
>
> When nitre (*potassium or sodium nitrate*) is applied to
> the root of a plant it will kill it as certainly as a knife mis-
> applied will kill a man; which proves that nitre is just as
> much food of plants as white arsenic is the food of rats.
>
> Every plant is earth and the growth and true increase
> of a plant is the addition of more earth.
>
> Rags of all sort are good (*in increasing plant growth*),
> one load being equal to about half a dozen of the best
> cow dung.
>
> Shrivelling of grain before harvest is 'one of the King-
> dom's curses' and is caused by "sinne."
>
> The soil is "the Pasture of the plant." The roots are
> "but guts inverted."

Chemistry Enters

The main obstacle in the early work was the existing
belief concerning the nature of matter. The ancient Greek
theory that everything is composed of air, water, earth, and
fire was over two thousand years old at the time but still
widely held. The loss of weight noted during burning was
considered due to loss of "phlogiston" to the air, and most
chemists spent their time trying to isolate and characterize
phlogiston.

With such a background the growth of chemical knowledge lagged and with it advancement in understanding of
plant nutrition. It was not until early chemists such as
Priestley, van Helmont, Cavendish, and Rutherford had
separated the gases we now know as oxygen, carbon dioxide, hydrogen, and nitrogen that further progress could be
made. These discoveries were made in the search for

phlogiston, however, and their application to plant nutrition was not recognized for many years.

The next step forward was made by Antoine Lavoisier, the brilliant French chemist of the latter eighteenth century, who finally overthrew the phlogiston theory by determining the real chemistry of combustion. Priestley and the others had made important discoveries but were still suffering from the phlogiston delusion and could not see the full value of their findings. Lavoisier could; he drew together the new knowledge, did his own checking by careful experiments, and evolved the new theory. One of his experiments illustrates his devotion to science. He and some fellow chemists went together and bought a diamond, which they proceeded to heat in a closed vessel until it disappeared—an expensive way of proving a point in their theory of combustion.

Lavoisier proved conclusively that when things burn oxygen is consumed and carbon dioxide and water are given off, part of the life cycle shown in Figure 1. He went further and by experiments undermined the theory of transmutation—from water to plant substance, for example—that had so long delayed the search for ultimate truth regarding chemical processes. Finally, he reached the conclusion that mass is never created or destroyed but that, if we can measure well enough, the weight of products is always found to equal the weight of the materials reacted. This concept, now so obvious and simple, is the law of conservation of mass, the foundation of modern chemistry.

In 1789 Lavoisier published his *Traité élémentaire de chemie* (*Elementary Treatise on Chemistry*), the first modern chemical textbook. He was still in the prime of life, only forty-six, and well equipped to drive forward a long way the budding science of chemistry. Five years later there took place one of the greatest tragedies of modern science; caught in the politics of the French Revolution, Lavoisier was sent to the guillotine. Joseph Louis Lagrange, the great mathematician, said: "It required only a moment to sever that head, and perhaps a century will not be sufficient to produce another like it." A different sentiment came from the petty judge who sentenced him: *"La République na pas besoin de savaats"* ("The republic does not need educated people").

Others began to follow the road that Lavoisier had charted and, in particular, to apply the new knowledge to study of plant growth. Jan Ingenhousz found that plants "purify the air," i.e., give off oxygen, but only in the presence of light. Then Jean Senebier, a Swiss natural philosopher, considered van Helmont's early crude experiments and concluded that the increase in weight of van Helmont's willow tree must have come from the air. However, it remained for René de Saussure, another Swiss, to prove by careful experiment in the early part of the nineteenth century that plants grow for the main part from atmospheric carbon dioxide and water supplied by the soil. This, plus Lavoisier's findings on the mechanism of combustion and decay, completes the photosynthesis circuit in Figure 1.

Notwithstanding de Saussure's careful work, he was questioned by some of his colleagues, particularly by Sir Humphry Davy in England. Sir Humphry, a distinguished scientist widely respected and quite effective in promoting agricultural chemistry as a separate science, agreed that carbon dioxide from the air was a plant food but argued that it was mainly absorbed by the soil and entered the plant through the roots. He was so enthusiastic about this theory that he recommended oil as a fertilizer because it contains carbon.

Davy's thinking on root absorption of carbon touched on another erroneous theory, already of some prominence, that decaying organic matter in the soil is the universal plant nutrient. This is the so-called "humus theory," now completely discredited in scientific circles but still set forth (sometimes with emotion) by the "organic gardening" school. It was a difficult theory to uproot because it was such a logical one to the early investigators; they felt that the products from decay of plant and animal material must be best suited for plant growth because they originally came from the plant. This thinking was not entirely bad because, as we have seen, the main constituents of plants do indeed recycle, but through the air-plant-air cycle of photosynthesis rather than the soil-plant-soil cycle of the humus theory.

All this helped explain the role of carbon dioxide and water but it did not touch very much on fertilization, which was already fairly well advanced in practice. Farmers generally realized the value of materials such as manure, ashes, and natural materials such as niter and applied them when obtainable. Theories as to why they helped, however, were about as confused as the early ones on the carbon dioxide-water-oxygen cycle.

De Saussure was interested in this also, particularly because when he burned plants there remained an ash that could not have been formed by carbon dioxide and water. Although his work was not conclusive he advanced several theories later proved valid (and exterminated some old ones):

    1. The soil furnishes a small part of the total plant substance, particularly the ash (mineral matter) and the nitrogen that makes up part of some compounds found in the plant.

    2. Plants do not spontaneously generate potash (an old theory).

    3. The plant roots do not take in soil as such, but act as selectively permeable membranes that allow a differential absorption of compounds dissolved in water.

4. Plant composition is not constant but varies with nature of the soil and age of the plant.

These concepts helped greatly in clarifying the situation and served as a solid foundation for further progress in the understanding of plant nutrition.

Liebig, Lawes, and Gilbert

At about the midpoint of the nineteenth century the sciences of chemistry and agronomy came together in the work of three men—Justus von Liebig in Germany and John Lawes and Henry Gilbert in England. Between them they worked out a good part of what is now known about plant nutrition and in so doing managed to start a controversy among agronomists—on the way plants take up nitrogen—that continued for over forty years.

Liebig was professor of chemistry at the University of Giessen from 1824 to 1852, during which time he investigated organic chemistry in general and plant growth processes in particular. In 1837 he addressed a British scientific society and presented his findings, which later were published under the title *Organic Chemistry in Its Application to Agriculture and Physiology,* perhaps the most important book ever published on the subject. Within eight years it had gone through seventeen editions and translations. One of the main contributions of the book was that it assembled all the knowledge available on plant nutrition and analyzed it in accordance with the best chemical science of the day. Liebig was well equipped to do this. He was the most noted chemist of the time, a brilliant writer and, incidentally, well able to take care of himself in an uninhibited era when investigators criticized each other freely. His conclusions can only be summarized in this brief review.

1. The plant gets most of its carbon from the air, by the action of green leaves in daylight.

2. Some carbon, a small part of the total, is taken up by the roots—from "carbonic acid" (carbon dioxide) formed by oxidation of soil organic matter.

3. Nitrogen comes from the air, where it occurs as ammonia, and is brought into the soil by rain.

4. Hydrogen and oxygen in the plant substance come from water. There is no need for organic matter (such as humus) to supply these elements.

5. All other elements needed by the plant, principally phosphorus and potassium, come from the soil, by a process of weathering insoluble soil minerals to give limited amounts of soluble compounds. Because of this slow rate of weathering, the supply must be increased by adding such compounds to the soil—that is, by applying fertilizer.

6. Chemical analysis of plant ash shows what the plant needs in the way of mineral elements (phosphorus, potassium, etc.) and analysis of the soil shows how much of these is available. Hence it is simple to determine how much fertilizer is needed.

7. Manure is useful only to the extent it contains minerals; the organic matter is unnecessary.

8. Bones are useful because they supply phosphate, and they are more effective if ground and even more so if treated with sulfuric acid.

Some of these conclusions have since been found erroneous but in the main they are a sound basis for plant nutrition as it is understood today. They were revolutionary, however, in Liebig's time. If he had not been such a distinguished scientist his ideas probably would have been ignored. They were accepted, however, at least in part, and Liebig subsequently did further work and published more books on fertilization.

The second of the great pioneers of the period, John

Bennet Lawes, was born in 1814 at Harpenden in Hertfordshire, near London. In 1837 he took charge of his father's estate, Rothamsted, and began to farm it. He had become interested in chemistry, and when Liebig came to England to deliver his famous lecture Lawes went to listen. He returned to Rothamsted and began a long series of experiments in chemistry and agriculture that contributed much to the early knowledge of plant nutrition.

The work Lawes began has continued to the present day, for Rothamsted is now the Rothamsted Experiment Station, one of the leading agricultural experiment stations of the world. The continuity from the early work of Lawes has been remarkable; records of crops grown on the Broadbalk Field, one of the Rothamsted experimental plots, are available from 1839 to date.

In 1843 Lawes employed Dr. Henry Gilbert, a chemist who had been trained under Liebig, to help him with the experimental work. The two men worked together for fifty-seven years in a painstaking and productive program of chemical and agronomic research.

The chemists and philosophers who explored the unknown area of plant nutrition in the years preceding the twentieth century made major contributions in a general way. But with the coming of research such as that of Liebig, Lawes, and Gilbert, the subject became much more complex. The course of inquiry was very much like that which has occurred in other fields: in the beginning there was much groping about and many wild theories proposed and vigorously supported; men like Liebig and his contemporaries evolved a valid basic theory but oversimplified it; and finally the very complex nature of the subject was recognized and a long, slow period of scientific exploration began. Today there are hundreds of laboratories and experiment stations studying problems of plant nutrition around the world, and thousands of researchers from many disciplines are working in the field. The basic principles in feeding of plants are well established and are sufficient to form an adequate basis for the giant fertilizer industry that grew up near the end of the first half of the twentieth century. A full understanding of the complex relationships between plant, soil, soil microorganisms (such as bacteria), and plant nutrients, however, has not yet been developed. In fact it might be said, as research opens up new vistas for exploration, that the search has only just begun.

The Nutrients Plants Need

The early work established that plants are composed mainly of carbon, hydrogen, and oxygen and that there is usually an unlimited supply of these in the atmosphere and in the soil. So if these elements were the only nutrients needed, then plants would almost always be well nourished. The earlier practical observations had shown, however, that plant growth is greatly stimulated by unknown constituents in manure, bones, and ashes, and experiments in the mid-nineteenth century demonstrated that carbon dioxide and water alone are not adequate for nutrition.

Liebig first proposed the theory that minerals added to the soil are plant nutrients of overriding importance. This was later termed "The Mineral Theory": "The crops on a field diminish or increase in exact proportion to the diminution or increase of the mineral substance conveyed to it in manure."[1] As mentioned earlier, Liebig thought that composition of the plant ash showed what mineral elements the plant needed and how much. Lawes and Gilbert disagreed with this and carried out experiments to

[1] "Manure" in this sense is anything applied to the soil to serve as plant food.

show that ash analysis is not an infallible guide to fertilization. They agreed, however, that the analysis is a qualitative indication of nutrient need.

One of the early contributors to this subject was Jean Baptiste Boussingault, a farmer in Alsace, who carried out numerous experiments involving growing of plants and analyzing them as a means of setting up a mineral balance sheet. He found phosphorus, sulfur, chlorine, calcium, magnesium, potassium, sodium, and silica in his tests, and later investigators added iron, manganese, and aluminum as elements usually found in plant ash. An example of the ash analysis for a particular crop, wheat, is as follows (in pounds of element per ton of dried plant material before ashing):

Potassium	10.5
Phosphorus	8.1
Calcium	1.1
Sulfur	5.2
Magnesium	3.1
Sodium	3.4
Chlorine	2.2

Hence the amount of mineral matter taken up by the plant from the soil is quite small in proportion to the carbon, hydrogen, and oxygen taken from the air and from the soil. From the above analysis, which includes most of the minerals in plant tissue that contribute significantly to the weight, the proportion is found to be about 1 to 60. So it is easy to see why van Helmont missed the uptake of soil minerals in his early willow tree experiment and concluded that water is the only material supplied by the soil.

Are all the mineral elements taken up by the plant really essential to growth? The early investigators assumed that they were and, as we have mentioned, that the amount taken up indicates the amount needed. Later work showed that neither of these concepts is completely true. It has been shown conclusively that the plant picks up some elements it can do without and more of some than it needs, a situation quite analogous to the way people eat.

It is not easy to define nutrient essentiality. The best criterion seems to be that an element is essential to optimum plant growth if (1) the plant will not fully mature if there is not enough of the element available, (2) the deficiency can be corrected only by supplying the particular element, and (3) the element is needed to improve the plant rather than to correct some adverse chemical or physical condition of the soil.

Based on this definition, thirteen elements other than carbon, hydrogen, and oxygen have been found essential for all plant growth situations: nitrogen (N), phosphorus (P), potassium (K), calcium (Ca), magnesium (Mg), sulfur (S), iron (Fe), manganese (Mn), copper (Cu), zinc (Zn), boron (B), molybdenum (Mo), and chlorine (Cl). Some of these are found in the plant in such minute quantities that they were not discovered until refined methods of plant analysis were developed; chlorine, for example, was not proven essential until 1954. With further improvement of analytical techniques, it may be that additional elements will be found essential.

In addition to these, other elements have been found helpful in some situations although they do not meet the full requirements for essentiality. Sodium, for example, can make up for a deficiency of potassium in some plants and is particularly helpful on saline (salty) soils. Silicon often gives a considerable yield increase for crops such as cereals that normally have a high silicon content in the plant tissue. And plants such as fungi appear to need beryllium, strontium, and several other rare elements; fungi are not of value as a crop, of course, but their nutrient needs are part of the overall subject of plant nutrition. Finally, elements such as arsenic, barium, bromine, cobalt, fluorine, iodine, lithium, nickel, selenium, and titanium, along with aluminum, are often found in plants. There is no present evidence that any of them are essential to plant growth.

We have seen earlier that the ash from wheat plants contains more phosphorus and potassium than other essential elements and that nitrogen, which burns out along with the carbon, hydrogen, and oxygen when the plant is ashed, is also a major element. These three—phosphorus, potassium and nitrogen—are so important in plant nutrition that they are called the *major nutrients*. Other elements, with a few exceptions, are present in the plant in much smaller proportions; the following tabulation gives some idea of the respective quantities removed from the soil by a crop, although it must be remembered that there is considerable variation in nutrient uptake by a particular type of plant, even in comparable crop growth situations.

		Nutrients in crop, lb./acre									
Crop	Yield per acre	N	P	K	Ca	Mg	S	Cu	Mn	Zn	B
Corn	100 bu.	90	15	21	6	6	7	0.04	0.06	0.10	
Sorghum	60 bu.	50	11	12	4	5	5	.01	.04	.04	
Apples	500 bu.	30	5	37	8	5	10	.03	.03	.03	0.01
Potatoes	400 bu.	80	13	120	3	6	6	.04	.09	.05	.05
Tomatoes	15 tons	90	13	11	5	8	10	.05	.10	.12	.14
Soybeans	40 bu.	150	15	43	7	7	4	.04	.05	.04	.01

These figures show the large need for nitrogen, greater than for any other nutrient except in crops such as apples and potatoes. They also show the reason for the general practice of classifying nutrients into three groups— *major* (or *macro*), *secondary,* and *micro.* Rough ranges for the amount of nutrient taken up by crops from an acre of soil are 10 to 150 pounds for nitrogen, phosphorus, and potassium (major nutrients), 1 to 10 pounds for calcium, magnesium, and sulfur (secondary nutrients), and 0.01 to 0.15 pound for all the others (micronutrients).

Resources in The Soil

One of the most difficult problems that faced the early investigators was how to evaluate the nutrients already in the soil. Whitney, in the United States, concluded that "the soil is the one indestructible immutable asset that the nation possesses. It is the one resource that cannot be exhausted, that cannot be used up . . . it cannot wear out, that so far as the mineral food is concerned it will continue automatically to supply adequate quantities of the mineral plant food for crops." Whitney considered fertilizers to be useful but not as sources of plant nutrient; he theorized that plants excrete poisonous substances toxic to succeeding crops and that the only function of fertilizers is to overcome this effect.

It seems strange now that this theory was widely held as late as 1911. When we consider the great amounts of nutrients present in the soil, however, it is easy to understand why the early workers could not see why more was necessary. The approximate range of nutrient content in soils is as follows (in pounds per acre in the upper 7 inches of soil):

Nitrogen	1000–6000
Phosphorus	800–2000
Potassium	Up to 49,000
Calcium	Up to 500,000
Magnesium	8000–26,000
Sulfur	Up to 3000
Boron	40–400
Chlorine	200–18,000

Copper	4–400
Iron	400 to over 200,000
Manganese	Up to 200,000
Molybdenum	About 4
Zinc	20–600

These amounts are enough for several years' supply for any crop, and for some nutrients enough for thousands of years. Nevertheless, it was proven early in history that continuous cropping and failure to return crop and animal residues to the soil causes a continual decrease in yield to a very low equilibrium level. In Europe, during the Dark Ages, the average yield of grain was only 6 to 10 bushels per acre.

Gradually the understanding developed that nutrient compounds in the soil are mainly insoluble and unavailable to plants. Natural processes such as weathering and microbial action dissolve some of these compounds slowly, but the rate is too slow for large yields when the fruit and grain are taken away from the soil and nutrients along with them. Return of manure helps but becomes more and more uneconomical as the cost of labor increases. Thus commercial fertilizers, while not absolutely essential to plant growth, are necessary in modern practice as supplements to the nutrient elements already present in the soil; the natural processes that cause soil minerals to become available are too slow for the high yields and production economy aimed for in modern crop production.

Nutrient Forms and Functions

How do plants use the minerals they mine from the soil? This simple question has been the subject of a vast amount of research, in laboratories, greenhouses, and field test plots all over the world, and the answer is not yet clear.

Some of the nutrients taken from the soil are needed

because they are essential constituents of chemical compounds formed in the plant tissue and later used by men and animals as food; for example, nitrogen is required in proteins. But starches, sugars, and fats require only carbon, hydrogen, and oxygen. Why, then, are all the other minerals taken up from the soil needed and how are they used? As will be discussed in more detail a little later, they enter into the complex chemistry of the plant in formation of intermediate compounds needed in synthesis of the end products. Others enter into compounds that have a variety of functions in the plant system, such as absorption and transfer of energy from the sun, moving materials through the plant, forming the woody part that serves as the plant "skeleton," and other functions not yet fully understood.

So far we have talked about nitrogen, phosphorus, potassium, manganese, and so on—as if the plant took up these in the elemental form. This cannot be, of course, any more than carbon or hydrogen could be taken up as such. All these are quite unpalatable to both plants and animals. A lump of coal, for example, contains carbon in the elemental form but it is not a good food; similarly, phosphorus in the elemental state is not a good fertilizer on two counts —it is poisonous to plants and it burns fiercely on exposure to air. All elements, then, with a few minor exceptions, must be supplied to plants as compounds of two or more elements—carbon, for example, as carbon dioxide (CO_2) and phosphorus as a compound such as dicalcium phosphate ($CaHPO_4$).

The compound selected to carry a particular nutrient must meet two main criteria: it must be soluble enough in the soil solution to feed the plant at an adequate rate, and it must not be poisonous to the plant.

The role of solubility is a puzzling one because it brings in the question of how the plant transfers nutrients from the soil to the roots, which remains one of the least understood areas of plant nutrition. Early theories ranged from transfer of the soil itself into the root interior (Jethro Tull in 1733) to the notion that the plant "drinks" water from the soil and thereby gets the nutrients incidentally in the drinking water. Both of these, the last of which is especially plausible, have been proven incorrect, but in their place we now have various theories, some conflicting, that also have not been proven. Soil colloids (extremely fine solid particles) are known to be important, as are complicated chemical processes such as adsorption (adherence to a surface) of ions on the root surface and ionic exchange between ions on the root surface and in solution.

This lack of conclusions about the method of nutrient uptake need not bother us, for it is clear that, whatever the mechanisms, the soil solution is essential as a transfer medium in moving nutrients to the root surface. For best efficiency, a fertilizer compound must be relatively mobile in the soil so that it can move from the fertilizer granule to the root, a distance that may be as much as several inches; dissolution in the soil solution gives it this mobility.

Some nutrient compounds are so poisonous to plants that they cannot be used, just as strychnine is poisonous to people even though it contains nitrogen. Others are acceptable if not supplied in too large an amount, just as too much salt (sodium chloride) can be quite harmful to animals. And some are satisfactory unless they are placed quite close or in contact with the root; if placed two inches or so away they become diluted by the soil water before they reach the root and the toxic effect of a concentrated solution on the plant is avoided.

Nitrogen was a particular problem to the early researchers in their efforts to understand the source and functions of nutrients. One of the peculiarities of the early period was that the logical conclusion—that nitrogen comes from the air along with carbon dioxide—does not appear to have been advanced, at least not with enough conviction to get into the literature. The reason possibly is that as late as 1813 Sir Humphry Davy held that nitrogen came from decaying animal and vegetable matter in the soil. In the meantime, late in the eighteenth century, the chemists were rapidly working out the chemistry of gases such as nitrogen, so that when Liebig gave attention to the problem it was already known that atmospheric nitrogen is a very inert gas that does not react with anything except when under extreme persuasion. Liebig had already disposed of Davy's (and others') "humus theory"—that all nutrients come from decaying organic matter—so when he considered alternatives he concluded that plants could not use atmospheric nitrogen because of its inertness.

Liebig's conclusion that nutrient nitrogen comes from ammonia (NH_3) present in the air is one of the major boners the great man committed. He even calculated that sources such as manure and decaying animals supply enough ammonia to the air that rainfall brings back about 60 pounds of ammonia per acre per year, sufficient for most crops.

Lawes and Gilbert did not agree with this at all. They caught all the rainwater falling on a measured area and found only about 5 pounds of ammonia per acre per year, a quantity quite inadequate for most crops. This started a controversy on source of nitrogen that lasted over forty years.

With humus, atmospheric nitrogen, and ammonia all pretty much discredited as nitrogen sources there was little else to turn to. Lawes and Gilbert thought there still might be some hope for atmospheric nitrogen; they started a long series of tests in England, and Jean Baptiste Boussingault, in France, joined in the effort. But after forty years of laborious effort Boussingault wrote Lawes that "If there is any fact perfectly demonstrated . . . it is this of nonassimilation of free nitrogen by plants." Lawes and Gilbert agreed and in 1882 reported failure in finding any solution to the problem.

One of the puzzling things was that experiments had verified the ancient observation that some plants grow well without manure and that in fields where these plants have grown, later crops of other kinds of plants grow as if the land had been fertilized. Boussingault found that legumes (plants such as clover and peas) accumulated nitrogen in the plant during growth, even in soil from which all organic matter had been carefully removed. Under the same conditions, there was no gain in nitrogen by wheat or oats.

In 1886 Hermann Hellriegel, in Germany, reported on experiments that finally solved the nitrogen problem. He grew peas in nitrogen-free soil and found that they turned yellow after the original nitrogen in the seed was used up. After a time most of the plants recovered their natural color and matured. An occasional plant failed to recover, however, and never reached full growth. Examination of the roots showed that the roots of the healthy plants were covered with many small nodules containing microorganisms whereas the occasional nonmaturing plants did not. It was also known that legumes generally have such root nodules but that other plants do not. Hellriegel concluded that the microorganisms (bacteria) convert elemental nitrogen to usable organic compounds of nitrogen and that the plant can then use these compounds as a source of nitrogen.

Hence Liebig and others were right. Plants do not use atmospheric nitrogen directly; they merely absorb it from the atmosphere and transfer it to the roots where the bacterial "factories" convert it to a usable form. To recapitulate, plants get nitrogen both from the air and the soil—by bacterial fixation from the air and from nitrogen compounds in the soil. The latter may be either fertilizers (manure or "chemical" fertilizer) added to promote growth or organic nitrogen compounds present in the soil as decomposition products of plants. Neither Liebig nor Davy were completely right or wrong on the humus theory; decaying vegetation does supply some nutrient to plants (which Liebig denied) but it is not an important source and certainly not the only one (which Davy held).

In view of bacterial fixation, why do we need nitrogen fertilizers? Legumes could be grown alternately with food crops to supply the nitrogen needed by both. The answer is that although legumes can be used effectively in agriculture to supply nitrogen, and still are to a considerable extent, the high yields sought in modern farming make nitrogen fertilizers indispensable. Legumes are sometimes undependable and also may not fix enough nitrogen for a succeeding crop, especially if the stalks and leaves are removed as a hay crop. Moreover, with the continuing reduction in cost of producing nitrogen fertilizers, it is often more economical to use fertilizer than to grow legumes, particularly since the land can then be used continuously for high-value crops.

Nitrogen is usually taken up from nitrogen compounds in the soil either as ammonium (NH_4^+) or nitrate (NO_3^-) ions that then combine with carbon compounds in the plant to form amino acids. These undergo further reactions to give either protein, the desired end product, or enzymes that act catalytically to bring about various reactions in the plant. As a constituent of protoplasm nitrogen is essential to the activity of every living cell. It makes up 16 to 18 percent of the weight of plant protein and 1 to 4 percent of the dry weight of plants.

The principal nitrogen fertilizers are ammonium nitrate (NH_4NO_3), ammonium sulfate [$(NH_4)_2SO_4$], and urea [$CO(NH_2)_2$]. Most plants take up nitrate (NO_3^-) more readily than ammonium (NH_4^+) or urea. For most agricultural situations, however, it makes little difference which form is used because the ammonium ion is converted rapidly to nitrate by the action of nitrifying bacteria in the soil. Urea travels a little longer route because it must first hydrolyze (react with water) to give ammonia and carbon dioxide before nitrification can take place. Other characteristics of these fertilizers will be discussed in later chapters.

Phosphorus is a very important element, first discovered by Henning Brand in Germany in 1669. Later workers discovered its importance as a necessary constituent of bones, a component of living cells, and an essential in nutrition of all living things. Its name was derived from the Greek words, *phos* (light) and *phore* (bearing). Since phosphorus glows in the dark the name is appropriate.

Liebig and the other early workers put phosphorus into a group with the other mineral elements. The situation was much simpler than for nitrogen; there was no possibility of the mineral elements coming from the air so the soil was the only possible source. Bones were already a time-honored fertilizer, although it was recognized that their efficiency was relatively low.

Phosphorus is taken up into the plant mainly as phosphate ion ($H_2PO_4^-$). The optimum concentration in the soil solution, as reported by several investigators, ranges from 0.2 to 0.7 parts per million. In the plant the phosphate has several functions. It is needed in conversion of starches to sugars; starch will form without phosphorus compounds present but does not readily convert to sugar without them. The element is also a constituent of the cell nucleus and is essential for cell division, formation of fat and albumen, and development of certain types of cell tissue.

The most important function, however, was discovered only recently. Certain high-energy phosphate chemical bonds have been found necessary in photosynthesis; these bonds apparently are necessary for transfer of energy in some of the processes essential to life of the plant.

Two main types of phosphate fertilizers are used, differing in the cation (positive part of the molecule) combined with the phosphate anion (negative part of the molecule). Calcium (Ca^{++}) and ammonium (NH_4^+) are the cations mainly used. Several compounds are involved because both calcium and ammonium can be combined with the phosphate in several ratios, each giving a compound with unique properties.

In contrast to nitrogen fertilizers, phosphates bring in the problem that the various phosphate fertilizer compounds normally used are not necessarily equally effective in promoting plant growth. The nitrogen fertilizers, with a few minor exceptions, are all about the same; all are readily soluble and available to plants. Phosphates, in contrast, vary in solubility and consequently in value as fertilizers.

Actually, the question is not so much one of solubility as of dissolving rate. As noted earlier, less than one part per million of phosphorus in the soil solution is enough to keep the plant fed adequately; even a very insoluble phosphate may be able to supply this much. The important consideration is that the fertilizer must be able to replenish the solution as fast as the plant takes up the phosphate. This is complicated by the fact that the plant takes up phosphate at widely varying rates during its life cycle, so that it is difficult to set any minimum acceptable dissolution rate for a phosphate fertilizer.

These considerations have led to much difference of opinion in evaluating phosphate fertilizers. Government agencies enter into this because practically all countries have laws providing that fertilizers be analyzed, by an official method, to make sure the farmer is getting the type of fertilizer he pays for. These methods are all based on the proportion of the fertilizer that dissolves in a given time under specified conditions of solvent type, temperature, and rate of stirring. Water is the solvent in some countries, but in most areas it is considered that this is too rigorous and that a more active solvent (usually an ammonium citrate solution of specified acidity) gives a better correlation with dissolution rate of the phosphate in the actual soil solution.

The fact that phosphate fertilizers must meet certain legal standards in regard to solubility has had an important effect on the course of process development in the field. Even if the fertilizer meets legal requirement for citrate solubility, however, most agronomists argue that it should also be at least partly water soluble; it is possible for a phosphate fertilizer to be fully citrate soluble but almost completely water insoluble. Probably the best solution would be to have a different official solvent for each type of phosphate fertilizer but legal requirements are difficult to change once they have been established; there has been some agitation in recent years to abandon the official citrate method but it has had little effect. One of the difficulties is that once an evaluation system is embedded in an industry, a change would hurt many companies that have invested money on the basis of the established system.

The most desirable solubility level depends on many factors that vary with the situation; high solubility is not necessarily good in all instances and low solubility is not necessarily bad. Much depends on the particle size of the fertilizer and on the pH (acidity) of the soil. For large particle size and low acidity (high pH) of soil, much higher solubility is needed than for fine particles and a highly acid soil (low pH).

To add to the confusion, soluble phosphate incorporated in the soil does not remain soluble very long. It dissolves in the soil solution but soon reacts with soil constituents such as calcium, magnesium, iron, and fluorine to form relatively insoluble precipitates. These in turn have some degree of solubility in the soil solution, and this "final" solution presumably is the source of phosphate for the plant roots. Or some of the original phosphate may pass into the root before it has time to precipitate from the soil solution.

This formation of a relatively insoluble precipitate, called "fixation" or "immobilization," is an important aspect of phosphate fertilization and has been studied in innumerable experiments. The situation is still not clear. The large number of variables involved make it very difficult to recommend anything generally applicable in the way of optimum fertilizer characteristics. It does appear, however, that fully water-soluble phosphate is least effective when it is used in finely divided form on acidic soils, since both promote immobilization. If the particle size is increased by granulation, the reduced surface area slows dissolution and subsequent immobilization, thereby making it more likely that the original phosphate will be present in the soil solution when the plant needs it. In contrast, high water solubility is desirable for high pH (basic) soils because immobilization reactions are not so prevalent and the rate of initial dissolution becomes the controlling factor. Phosphates of low solubility do best when finely divided and used on acid soil because, again, rate of solution tends to be more important than immobilization.

The general trend is toward larger particle size of fertilizers (granulation), a factor that makes high solubility desirable. Also, in modern fertilizer practice high soil acidity is avoided by application of lime. Thus it may be said that the trends favor higher water solubility of phosphate; on the other hand, present conditions probably do not warrant a requirement of water solubility higher than, say, 50 percent. The level of fertilization is also important, since low solubility has less adverse effect when the soil already contains a relatively large amount of phosphate. A final conclusion is hard to draw; the best that can be said is that 50 percent water solubility is satisfactory for most situations at present but that the level probably will increase in the future.

Potassium is a much less complex fertilizer element than nitrogen or phosphorus. It clearly is taken up from the soil, there are no complex solubility problems as there are with phosphorus, and potash compounds suitable for use with little processing can be mined from vast deposits scattered over the world. If all the plant nutrients were as easy to obtain and use, and as free of complications in regard to uptake by the plant, fertilization would be a simple subject indeed.

The function of potassium in plant growth, however, is a more complex question. It is not known definitely to be a constituent of plant protoplasm, as are nitrogen and phosphorus. It occurs in the plant mainly as a soluble inorganic salt in the plant tissues or sometimes as part of the anion of organic acids. It seems to be important in formation and movement of carbohydrates in the plant; a deficiency of potassium quickly lowers the carbohydrate content. Another function appears to be that of promoting conversion of amino acids to protein, for a potassium deficiency results in accumulation of amino acids in the plant.

Although its functions are obscure, potassium is essential for vigorous plant growth and resistance to disease. It is required in relatively large amounts, sometimes approaching the need for nitrogen; the content in plants generally ranges from 0.5 to 2.5 percent of the dry plant weight.

The usual commercial fertilizer is potassium chloride, a

soluble compound that can be used without further processing after it is mined and purified.

Calcium functions not only as a plant nutrient but also
as a soil amendment to correct soil acidity. The need for
"liming" the soil was recognized early in the history of agriculture; the early Greeks dug up marl (soil containing
calcium carbonate) for this purpose. In the plant it is a
major constituent of the cell walls in leaves. Unlike the
macronutrients, it does not move readily in the plant, so
there is little movement from old to younger growth when
a deficiency occurs. The exact function is not well understood, but a deficiency prevents normal development of
buds and root tips.

The small amount of calcium needed by plants usually
is supplied adequately by the many calcium compounds
present in the soil. For this reason supplying of calcium is
not part of the fertilizer industry. Some fertilizers contain
calcium but only incidentally, because it is the cation associated with nutrient-bearing anions such as nitrate and
phosphate. Large amounts of calcium carbonate are applied to the soil to correct acidity but this is a local mining
and grinding operation—not associated with the fertilizer
industry.

Magnesium has the unique distinction of being the only
mineral constituent of chlorophyll, and this seems to be its
main function in the plant. It makes up almost 3 percent
of the weight of the chlorophyll but must be present in
considerably larger amounts to maintain the chlorophyll
in good operating condition. Other functions in the complex chemistry of the plant have also been identified.

Most soils contain enough available[1] magnesium compounds to supply plant needs. When a deficiency is found,

[1] Availability in this sense relates to characteristics of the nutrient compound that make it possible for the plant to take up the
nutrient.

dolomitic limestone (containing $MgCO_3$) can be used to supplement the natural supply. Again, this is a local type of operation and the supplying of magnesium is not usually regarded as a function of the fertilizer industry.

Sulfur is important in plant chemistry because it is a constituent of many plant proteins, especially in the form of amino acids that in some instances contain over 25 percent sulfur. Moreover, there is a recent theory that a particular compound in the plant, 6, 8-thioctic acid [$SSCH_2CH_2CH(CH_2)_4COOH$], has an extremely important function, for the connecting bond between the two sulfur atoms may be the point at which radiant energy from the sun is converted to chemical energy. If this is true then sulfur is a most important plant nutrient.

The sulfur needs of the plant are relatively small in quantity and can be supplied from at least three sources. There are usually compounds in the soil, mainly organic types, that are broken down by natural processes to give available sulfur; industrial waste gases that contain sulfur compounds distribute them over the landscape; and, finally, many fertilizers contain sulfates that supply sulfur incidentally.

Even with these varied sources, however, there is often not enough sulfur for plant needs; every year new areas are found where plants start turning yellow because of sulfur starvation. The supplying of sulfur is more and more becoming a significant function of the fertilizer industry.

Boron, one of the more important of the micronutrients, is another of the elements whose function is not well understood. It seems to have a part in protein synthesis. The term "micronutrient" is quite suitable for boron because too much is as bad as too little; an excess amount, which is not far above the minimum for good nutrition, is toxic to plants.

Like other micronutrients, deficiencies are developing in more and more areas and the demand for boron compounds in commercial fertilizers is growing.

Iron is used by the plant in various enzyme processes. It is also known to be essential in chlorophyll formation but does not remain in the chlorophyll molecule. There is so much iron in the soil (combined in various ways) that adding more is seldom required. In some areas and for some crops, however, the soil can be heavily loaded with iron compounds without supplying much to the plant. This is particularly true for citrus grown in Florida, where special organic compounds containing iron in an available form are often applied.

Zinc is also involved in some of the enzyme processes and, like boron, is toxic if too much is applied. And also like boron, the growing deficiency in soils is increasing the importance of zinc compounds as fertilizers.

Manganese seems to act mainly as an oxidizing agent in plants. Some deficient areas have been noted but the element is not as important in fertilization as boron and zinc.

Copper probably is another of the nutrients that take part in enzyme systems, and can be quite toxic if too much is used. It is relatively unimportant as a fertilizer.

Molybdenum was one of the last nutrient elements found to be essential; the delay was mainly because only a relatively few molecules can be found in the plant. Its role is not understood. Application in fertilizers is seldom required, but when there is a deficiency addition of molybdenum can give dramatic results.

Chlorine has recently been proven essential but its function is unknown. A very small amount helps crops such as alfalfa and tobacco but even a moderate amount is bad for growth and quality of potatoes and tobacco. Chlorine is not a commercial fertilizer nutrient because the small amounts needed are supplied by the soil or by incidental compounds in fertilizers.

The Economic Question

In the early days of agriculture—the manure and ashes era—the cost of farming was not given much thought. There was little or no outlay of cash; the farmer grew his own seed, supplied his own fertilizer, and provided motive power in the form of horses (or bullocks) and his own muscles. The farm was a family operation, a self-contained enterprise.

In some areas of the world this is still the rural way of life, but it is fast passing away, even in the less developed countries. In the more advanced areas, much of the crop production is on large farms operated on a "food factory" basis. Seed is bought from specialty growers; tractors, combines, and other machines make it possible for one or two men to farm hundreds of acres; and large amounts of fertilizer are bought and used to give high yields per acre.

On such farms, the cost of every input is carefully scrutinized, just as in any efficient manufacturing operation. One of the more important factors is choice of fertilizer type.

Selection of the fertilizer to use is affected by many factors, but agronomic effectiveness is seldom one of them. This anomalous situation comes about because over the history of plant nutrition several good materials have been developed, all of them good fertilizers. Except in special cases one is about as effective as the other. Hence the farmer can base his choice on the very important factor of cost, measured in terms of overall cost per unit of nutrient, of fertilizer applied to the soil.

The next decision is how much fertilizer to use, which is not an easy question because it depends on considerations such as (1) the amount of nutrients already in the soil (natural fertility), (2) the nutrient requirement of the crop being grown, which differs among plant types and (3) the economic return that can be expected per unit of nutrient applied. Some gambling may also be involved; in semiarid areas, for example, the fertilizer investment may be lost in a dry year when lack of water is the controlling factor. In such a situation the farmer may choose to use less than the optimum amount of fertilizer in order to reduce the risk.

Since soil fertility and crop type are fixed for a particular farming situation, the main variable is *profit per unit of fertilizer nutrient applied*. It is obvious that there is some limit to the amount of fertilizer that can be used economically. A given amount of fertilizer, say fifty pounds per acre, will increase crop yield by a certain amount, but as we apply additional increments of fifty pounds the yield increase from each increment becomes smaller and smaller until a point is reached at which the cost of the fertilizer increment becomes larger than the value of the increase in yield resulting from it. In practice the application should be stopped somewhere before this—at a point beyond which the yield increase no longer is large enough to give an adequate profit on the investment in the fertilizer increment. This can be more easily understood from actual figures on fertilizer cost and value of increased yield.

	Nitrogen applied (lb./acre)				
	0	40	80	120	160
Average corn yield, bu.	26	54	74	85	91
Yield increase per increment, bu.	–	28	20	11	6
Value of increase (at $2.00/bu.), $	–	56.00	40.00	22.00	12.00
Cost of fertilizer per increment, $	–	5.85	5.85	5.85	5.85

Here the return on investment was very high, almost $9.00

profit for each dollar spent, for the first forty pounds of nitrogen. The last forty pounds, however, only returned about one dollar for each one invested; this is still a good return and another forty pounds might have been profitable, but with the uncertainties of whether the farmer might wish to stop while his chances of profit were still high.

These yield increases are from actual crop growth tests on particular fields; in some other year (with different weather) and at some other location the results likely would have been different. Hence prediction of yield increase per unit of fertilizer, as a means of determining the optimum amount of fertilizer to use, must be based on the farmer's experience with his own soil; at best only a rough guess can be made.

Even if the farmer can make a good guess as to the most economical amount of fertilizer, he does not necessarily use this much. As with other businessmen, his capital is often limited. He has several ways in which he can invest it and some of these may be more profitable than purchase of fertilizer. Quite often the money for fertilizer must be borrowed, with the expected crop as security, and adequate credit may not be available on this basis. Efficient farmers, however, make every effort to apply the optimum amount of fertilizer, for otherwise the full potential profit from the farming operation cannot be realized.

The amount of fertilizer used by farmers around the world varies widely.

Countries like Holland and Japan, who must farm intensively to feed their dense populations, use the most fertilizer per acre. The major powers, the United States and U.S.S.R., use much less because agriculture is not well advanced in some parts of these very large countries and the great acreage available takes some of the emphasis off intensive farming. And in the less-developed areas such as Africa and India very little fertilizer is used, even though

Amount of nutrient used, lb./acre, 1961

	Nitrogen	Phosphate	Potash	Total
Holland	192	95	119	406
Japan	111	73	88	272
West Germany	65	68	104	237
Taiwan	107	38	37	182
United Kingdom	56	52	55	163
South Korea	94	24	3	121
France	24	37	31	92
United States	13	12	10	35
U.S.S.R.	3	3	3	9
Africa	1	1	0.5	2.5
India	1.5	0.3	0.2	2

food production is critically low; both the backwardness of the farmers and their lack of capital keep them from using the best tool they have for raising more food. Many of these farmers use no fertilizer at all.

In Summation

The science of plant nutrition is complicated and sometimes confusing—let us summarize.

1. Although in the past there have been long and sometimes heated arguments on the matter, it is now clear that plants take up nutrients, with the exception of carbon dioxide, through their roots.

2. The actual mechanism of nutrient uptake is still not clear but the soil solution is highly important, presumably because it dissolves nutrients and carries them to the root surfaces.

3. Nitrogen, phosphorus, and potassium, generally termed the major nutrients (or macronutrients), are the most important ones. The main function of the fertilizer industry is to supply them.

4. Calcium, magnesium, and sulfur, the secondary nutrients, are important but are not of major importance in the fertilizer industry. In most cases they are either already available in the soil in adequate amount or are present incidentally in fertilizers.

5. The micronutrients—boron, manganese, zinc, copper, iron, and molybdenum—are growing in importance as fertilizer nutrients but the small amounts required give them limited commercial significance.

6. There are vast amounts of plant nutrients already provided by nature—such as nitrogen in the air and many compounds in the soil. The plant can make use of these, in one way or another, which is why plants can grow without the use of fertilizers. Nature's course is slow, however—too slow for the high yields needed in modern agriculture. So manufactured fertilizers, rapidly and immediately available to the plant, are essential.

7. Because of their chemical properties most of the nutrients cannot be used as such in their elemental form. Nitrogen works best in the ammonium (NH_4^+), nitrate (NO_3^-), or urea [$(NH_2)_2CO$] forms, and is usually supplied as ammonium sulfate [$(NH_4)_2SO_4$], ammonium nitrate (NH_4NO_3), or urea [$(NH_2)_2CO$]. Phosphorus is used only in the phosphate form (PO_4^{3-}) and is supplied mainly as ammonium phosphate or calcium phosphate. Potassium is the easiest of the three to supply, for it occurs naturally as potassium chloride (KCl), a good fertilizer that requires no further processing.

8. The action and function of the various nutrients in the plant is one of the least understood phases of plant nutrition. Plant growth tests, however, show that all the nutrients we have listed are essential to healthy plant growth.

9. A small amount of fertilizer will almost always return its cost many times over by increasing yield. As the amount is increased, however, each increment gives less yield increase, until the point is reached at which the yield increase is not high enough to pay for the last

fertilizer increment. The efficient farmer estimates the expected increase in yield and uses the amount of fertilizer that will give maximum profit.

10. Since many farmers do not operate their farms in a businesslike way, and some lack capital, the amount of fertilizer used is often less than the optimum. Because of ignorance, many farmers, particularly in underdeveloped areas, use little or no fertilizer. Average amounts used range from over 400 pounds of nutrient per acre in Holland to only about 2 pounds in India.

CHAPTER 3

The Fertilizer Industry

The word "fertilizer" is related to fertility, which in turn comes from the Latin word *ferre,* to bear. The fertility of the soil, and its ability to bear crops, has always been an important consideration in the history of man. As soon as the early farmers learned that manure, bones, and ashes made the soil more fertile they began conserving such materials and using them to increase crop production. Then, as specialization became a part of community economy, the practice of selling fertilizer materials began.

The fertilizer industry, which may be defined as manufacture and sale of fertilizer, had its beginnings a long time ago. Perhaps the earliest manufacture was by the Chinese, who are said to have calcined bones for use as fertilizer some two thousand years ago. Or early entrepreneurs who mined and crushed saltpeter may have the best claim to being first. In any event, by 1786 there were mills in England grinding bones to increase their fertilizer effectiveness.

All of these were relatively simple operations, far removed from today's chemical type of fertilizer manufacture. The first chemically-produced fertilizers appeared during the midpart of the nineteenth century. For a long time it was considered that Liebig first proposed such a fertilizer and that Lawes, in England, was the first to produce it. It now appears, however, that this is an injustice to Kohler, in Austria; modern historical research shows that Kohler treated bones with sulfuric acid in 1831 to make them more soluble. He apparently did not get much publicity, for Liebig's proposal in 1840 to do the same thing was regarded for over a hundred years as the beginning of the fertilizer industry. In 1843 Lawes, following the lead of Liebig, began commercial production of a fertilizer made by treating coprolites, a phosphate ore, with sulfuric acid.

Lawes' new fertilizer rapidly became popular because it gave much higher yields than untreated bones or phosphate ore. The product, generally called superphosphate, was a good one and is still the leading phosphatic fertilizer of the world. The process is somewhat unique in chemical history, for it is still carried out very much as it was when Lawes first started production. More efficient equipment is used today but the process steps are much the same.

From this beginning the manufacture of superphosphate spread fairly rapidly. Other plants were built in Europe and the first recorded sale of superphosphate took place in the United States in 1852. Plants were small, however, and annual production was not very large even as late as the 1920s.

Nitrogen fertilizers developed more slowly. There was not as much incentive, for the manures and other organic materials used in early farming practice were good suppliers of nitrogen—in contrast to bones and phosphate ore, which are not very effective fertilizers unless treated with acid to increase solubility.

Mining of the first inorganic nitrogen fertilizer, sodium nitrate, began in Chile in the early 1800s; the first shipment to the United States arrived in 1830. The nitrate deposits in Chile are unique. Their origin is unknown, although several theories have been advanced. Their very existence is an unusual circumstance, because sodium nitrate is so soluble that one would expect rainfall to dissolve it quickly. But the deposit lies in a desert valley, between the coastal mountains and the Andes, where the rain never falls.

In this forbidding region there was built up in the latter part of the nineteenth century a thriving mining and processing industry. A considerable amount of processing was required, because the sodium nitrate occurs as a mixture with several other materials, requiring several dissolving and crystallizing steps to remove the impurities.

Sodium nitrate production in 1850 was only 30,000 tons per year but by 1880 had risen to a million tons, a large amount of fertilizer for those days. Production continued to increase as world consumption of fertilizer grew, reaching a maximum of 3,500,000 tons in 1929. Then, as often happens in the chemical industry, the material began to lose favor as new nitrogen fertilizers with better properties came into use. Production of sodium nitrate in 1965 was about 1,200,000 tons and its contribution to world fertilizer nitrogen use was only 2 percent.

Potash has followed much the same chronology of development as nitrogen and phosphate. During the period 1839–43, German miners drilling for salt (sodium chloride) near Stassfurt found a bed of potassium chloride and sulfate. Liebig was studying the effect of potassium compounds on plant growth at the time, and interest in his work led to development and use of the Stassfurt deposits. German potash became the principal world source and remained so until 1940. During World War I the curtailed supply led to exploration in the United States and a beginning of production. The situation was so critical in the United States during this period that potassium chloride sold as high as $500 per ton; the price today is only about $35.

In 1926 Congress appropriated $500,000 for potash exploration in the United States. Great deposits were found. Today the United States leads the world in potash production—over 2,500,000 tons in 1966.

All this leads us to the 1920s and 1930s, a period of major change in the fertilizer industry. By this time many of the older sources of nitrogen and phosphate were be-

ginning to fall behind. A group of new fertilizers, of higher
nutrient content and better physical properties, had their
beginnings and early growth in this period and the increasing awareness by farmers that fertilizers are profitable led
to rapid growth in fertilizer consumption. In 1856 fertilizer
use in the United States was less than 100,000 tons; by
1900 the figure had risen to 2,200,000 tons and in 1950
American farmers used 17,989,000 tons of fertilizer.

In the century 1850–1950 the fertilizer industry
changed gradually from a simple to a relatively complex
technology. Although treatment of phosphate ore with sulfuric acid was a type of chemical manufacture, it was carried out by the early producers in crude equipment and
mainly by hand labor. This changed gradually to equipment more complicated and efficient, continuous or semi-
continuous operation, and mechanization to reduce the
manpower required. Instead of the mining of nitrate ores
or recovering of ammonia from coke-oven gas (another
early practice), synthesis of ammonia from atmospheric
nitrogen, a very sophisticated technology, moved into a
leading position in nitrogen supply. And many other
chemical processes, which we shall describe later, became
significant in the fertilizer field.

The 1950s and 1960s make up another period in which
major changes took place in the industry. Products that
were of little consequence in 1950 became major nutrient
suppliers, trends in consumption of several of the older
materials reversed, new physical forms of fertilizer became popular, and consumption took another sharp upward
turn (to an estimated 37,000,000 tons in the United States
in 1967, an increase of over 100 percent since 1950; see
Fig. 2). Fertilizer producers became much more research
conscious as the great plant nutrient needs of the future
became more evident. The same future potential brought
new types of producers into the field, companies generally

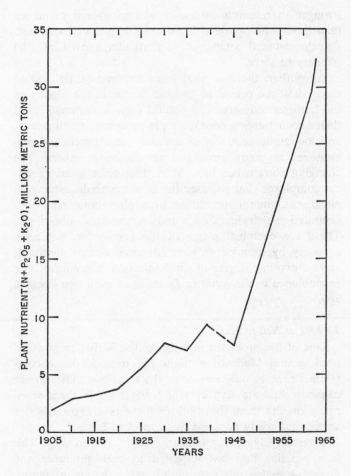

Fig. 2 World consumption of fertilizer has more than doubled since 1950 and is still growing rapidly. The fastest growing nutrient is nitrogen, now increasing at a rate that would double consumption every ten years.

stronger in research capability and in overall resources than those who operated the simpler industry of the past. Petroleum-based companies, in particular, moved into the industry in force.

Altogether, there is good basis for terming the period since 1950 the period of greatest change in the history of the fertilizer industry. The natural organic materials (and their accompanying odor), simple processes, small plants, and low-grade products of the past have practically disappeared in many areas and are fading in others. The changing pattern has brought in their place great chemical complexes that produce the new materials—ammonia, nitric acid, ammonium nitrate, urea, phosphoric acid, concentrated superphosphate, and ammonium phosphate. These are chemical plants of the first order, achieving economy by tremendous size, advanced control methods, and an extreme degree of mechanization. They have little resemblance to the fertilizer factories of even two decades ago.

To Mix or Not to Mix

One of the problems in fertilizer use is that most crops need several kinds of nutrient but most fertilizer compounds contain only one or at the most two. The farmer can buy separate fertilizers and either apply them separately or mix them, but both of these take extra labor, a scarce and costly commodity on modern farms.

Alternatively, the producer can do the mixing. This is a practice that has appealed to both producer and farmer; it makes profit for both because the manufacturer, with his large-scale operation, can do the mixing at lowest cost.

Production of mixed fertilizers began over a hundred years ago. In a typical early operation, the fertilizer producer would buy phosphate ore, sulfuric acid, sodium nitrate, and potassium chloride; mix the acid and phosphate to make superphosphate; mix the superphosphate, sodium nitrate, and potassium chloride together; and market the mixture. In the beginning the mixes were probably made to prescription, that is, the farmer specified the proportions of nitrogen, phosphate, and potash that he wanted in the mix. This he could do because fertilizer plants were small and often served only one community, so the farmer could drive his wagon to the plant.

As fertilizer operations became larger they had to serve a larger area to move the product, and it became convenient for the producer to ship the fertilizer to the farmer rather than for the farmer to go get it. Also, it became inconvenient to make up mixes to order; production cost could be lowered by running the plant for an extended period on a certain mix and then shifting to another one. Now the producer selected the nutrient proportions rather than the farmer. But to keep his customers happy he made the mixes that he thought most of the farmers would want.

This was the beginning of the mixed fertilizer industry, which has grown until today well over half the fertilizer used is purchased in the mixed form.

One of the first problems was how to describe a particular mixture so that the farmer could identify it. Giving the pounds of superphosphate, sodium nitrate, and potassium chloride going into a ton of mix would have been too cumbersome, so the custom developed of giving the nutrient percentages—which was quite logical because the farmer was paying his money for the nutrient elements rather than the calcium, sodium, oxygen, and chlorine associated with them. Thus a certain mixture might be described and advertised as a 5-10-10, meaning that it contained 5 percent nitrogen (N), 10 percent phosphate (P_2O_5), and 10 percent potash (K_2O).

Fertilizer mixtures do not contain P_2O_5 and K_2O as

such, of course. Potassium chloride, for example, contains no oxygen at all; the K_2O equivalent is arrived at by calculation. It would have been much more logical and convenient to have used the phosphorus (P) and potassium (K) contents, to put these on the same basis as nitrogen (N), but the early fertilizer investigators for some reason adopted the oxide basis and it remains firmly embedded in the industry today. Actually, nitrogen was not expressed as such in the early days, but rather as ammonia (NH_3). The industry was able to get away from this in the early part of the present century, but not away from the oxides.

Today there is a major effort under way by agronomists and others to adopt the elemental basis of reporting nutrient content. One of the difficulties, not very important but showing the illogical nature of oxide reporting, is that some of the new materials being investigated are so concentrated that the nutrient content adds up to over 100 percent on the oxide basis. Products made by reacting ammonia with phosphorus and air, for example, may be as high as 15-90-0 (the zero indicates no potash), or a total (N plus P_2O_5) of 105 percent, obviously impossible. The elemental basis would give 15-39-0, which is both reasonable and accurate.

It is quite difficult to change an established commercial custom, however, because the whole system is based on it and great expense and inconvenience result if any change is attempted. It is much like changing from driving on the left to driving on the right, or from the English system of measurement to the metric.

Like any very old technology, the fertilizer industry has terms and expressions that are peculiar to it. One of these, used mainly in the mixed fertilizer industry, is "grade." Grade of a fertilizer is the nutrient content, expressed on the $N-P_2O_5-K_2O$ basis as we have seen. Thus we have a 5-10-10 grade, a 10-5-5 grade, and so on. Low grade does not mean that the fertilizer is a poor one but that the nutrient content is relatively low.

Fertilizer producers ordinarily manufacture several grades, depending on the customer demand. They may also make a certain grade and advertise it for a specific use, such as "tobacco fertilizer" or "vegetable fertilizer." This practice is declining, however, as farmers become more sophisticated and take into account the more important consideration that the land they want to fertilize has unique and specific nutrient needs, as shown by soil analysis.

The whole system of grades has gotten somewhat out of hand. Producers have originated grades to give them something different to sell, and many farmers, from one source or another, have gained the impression that certain particular grades have intrinsic superior properties. As a result over three thousand different grades are made in the United States. Manufacture of this many grades complicates production and increases cost, and is unnecessary because agronomists generally agree that a relatively few grades would cover practically all the needs.

Again, this problem is fading as farmers become better informed. Moreover, several states have regulations limiting and specifying the grades that can be sold.

Up until the period of innovation that began about 1920, practically all mixed fertilizers were made, as the name implies, simply by mechanical mixing of various materials. In the 1920s and early 1930s, products came into use that contained nitrogen and phosphate chemically combined. One of them, ammoniated superphosphate, became so popular that in the period bounded roughly by 1935 to 1955 it was the most important supplier of phosphate to mixed fertilizers. Superphosphate is acidic in nature and will absorb ammonia. When the new ammonia industry of the 1920s made ammonia available, fertilizer producers soon adopted ammoniation of superphosphate as an economical practice.

Ammonium phosphate, made by reacting ammonia with phosphoric acid, also had its beginnings in this period. It was somewhat early for its time, however, and did not become popular until after 1950, when its adoption became one of the outstanding features in the changing structure of the industry.

Another of the "chemically mixed" products is nitric phosphate, made by dissolving phosphate ore in nitric acid and neutralizing the resulting slurry with ammonia. This was also first produced in the 1930s, in Germany, and, like ammonium phosphate, has become important since 1950. The product is especially popular in Europe, less so in the United States.

All these are chemical combinations containing nitrogen and phosphate. Potash, because natural potassium chloride is so economical, has offered little promise for chemical combinations. In the 1960s, however, production of potassium nitrate began, made by reacting potassium chloride with nitric acid. Production so far is relatively small.

These chemically mixed products are both used as is and in mixes with other materials; for example, a mixture of ammoniated superphosphate, ammonium sulfate, and potassium chloride was a major product for many years in the 1935–55 period. A combination of ammonium phosphate, ammonium sulfate, and potassium chloride, mixed together and the mixture then agglomerated, is a leading fertilizer today.

It is interesting to note that fertilizer mixing, which began as a local operation, has to some extent gone full cycle. One of the more important fertilizer developments of recent years is "bulk blending," a local operation in which fertilizer materials are mixed mechanically, often to order. The reasons for this will be elaborated in a later chapter.

The antithesis of mixed fertilizer is "straight fertilizer," a term applied to a fertilizer material that goes from the original manufacture to the farmer without any mixing with anything else in between. These are the products that we have mentioned before—ammonium nitrate, urea, ammonium sulfate, superphosphate, ammonium phosphate, and potassium chloride. Although farmers use more mixed than straight fertilizer, there are special farming situations that require the straight type. For example, plants need frequent feeding with nitrogen since it contributes so heavily to stalk and leaf growth, so farmers often apply a straight nitrogen fertilizer alongside the growing plant once or twice during the growing season. A straight potash fertilizer may also be applied to pastures because potash need not be applied as frequently as nitrogen and phosphate.

Straight fertilizers are often designated as certain grades, in the same way as for mixed fertilizers, particularly when the fertilizer is of the binutrient, chemically mixed type. Ammonium phosphates, for example, may be 16-20-0, 16-48-0, 18-46-0, and so on. Single nutrient products may be referred to in the same way, although there is much less reason for it. Thus ammonium nitrate becomes 33.5-0-0, urea 45-0-0, ammonium sulfate 21-0-0, superphosphate 0-20-0 (or 0-45-0 for concentrated superphosphate), and potassium chloride 0-0-60.

High Analysis and Granulation

In the early decades of fertilizer production, nutrient concentration received little attention. The products were quite dilute but there was little producers could do about it because the only materials available to them were low grade. The superphosphate contained so much moisture that the P_2O_5 content was often as low as 15 percent; sodium nitrate, diluted by the sodium and oxygen in the molecule, contained only 16 percent nitrogen; and even the potash material was relatively low in concentration, as low as 20 percent K_2O, because unrefined ore containing sodium chloride was used. With such materials the limit for an equinutrient grade was 5-5-5, very low by today's standards.

The low grade was not a great problem in the early days when the fertilizer was made near where it was to be used. But as larger plants were built and the fertilizer was shipped farther, the cost of shipping useless diluents such as the calcium, oxygen, and chlorine portions of molecules became a major drawback. Little was done about it, however, until the 1920–40 period brought in more highly concentrated fertilizer compounds. In the industry this is called the trend to "high analysis," another of the terms peculiar to the field.

The new materials reduced shipping and handling costs but they brought a new problem with them. Almost without exception, they were more hygroscopic than the old ones, that is, they picked up moisture more rapidly from the air. Moisture absorption not only makes fertilizers moist and sticky but also causes them to cake. During a period of high humidity moisture is taken up and then when humidity drops it dries out again. But the moisture dissolves some of the fertilizer as it is absorbed. The resulting solution, which forms a film on the fertilizer particles, crystallizes when the fertilizer dries out again, and the crystals cake the fertilizer by knitting particles together.

Fertilizer caking is one of the most serious problems in modern fertilizer technology. The way of economy has led to higher and higher concentration but this in turn has made the physical properties worse. Various means have been used to deal with the problem but the most effective by far has been granulation, that is, agglomerating small particles to make larger ones. Prior to the granulation era, no attempt was made to alter particle size during fertilizer manufacture. As a result the particles were usually fairly small and subject to severe caking. Granulation to increase particle diameter reduces surface area, thus providing fewer granule contact points at which crystal bridges can form. A simple analogy is wetting of clay and gravel; drying cakes the clay but the gravel is not affected.

Size of granules produced varies with fertilizer type and the area where it is used. The bulk of granular fertilizer probably falls in the range of 8 to 20 mesh, which means that none of the particles are caught on a screen made up of fine wires spaced 8 to the inch but all are caught on one with 20 wires to the inch. Particle size is specified as a range of mesh size because granulation methods are not precise enough to give particles all of the same size; hence the mesh size range is a measure of the largest and smallest particles in the mass.

Granulation has allowed a major increase in fertilizer nutrient content. With urea (45-0-0), diammonium phosphate (18-46-0), and potassium chloride (0-0-62), it is now possible to make a 20-20-20 grade, a long way from the 5-5-5 made from sodium nitrate, superphosphate, and unrefined potassium chloride in early fertilizer history. The average nutrient content of all fertilizer has risen steadily over the past sixty years (see Fig. 3).

The first of the high-analysis mixed fertilizers was a product called Nitrophoska, made in Germany in the early 1930s. A granular mixture of ammonium nitrate, diammonium phosphate, and potassium chloride, the product was ahead of its time. Only a small tonnage was made,

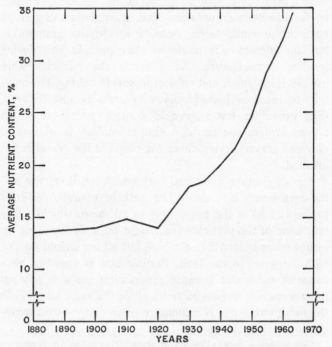

Fig. 3 The average nutrient content of fertilizers in the United States has increased almost threefold since 1880.

and similar high-analysis mixes were not produced again until the 1950s.

Solid, Liquid, or Gas

Most people assume that fertilizers are solid materials, which is a correct assumption for most of fertilizer history. About the only exception was use of nitrogen materials in liquid form in the midnineteenth century. The amount was small, however, and never became significant.

Starting about 1950 other physical forms came into use. Probably the most radical innovation ever made in fertilizer use technology was introduction of ammonia as a fertilizer, which, in effect, was use of fertilizer in a gaseous form. Ammonia is a gas at ordinary temperature and pressure, and although it is handled and shipped as a liquid under pressure, it becomes a gas again when released through applicator nozzles into the soil.

Using a pressurized liquid as a fertilizer, with the attending hazard of working with pressure equipment, was a long step forward for farmers, particularly since escaping ammonia can injure or kill. But the new material was readily accepted and in fifteen years grew from almost nothing to the position of leading nitrogen fertilizer in the United States, a forceful evidence of the rapidly increasing capability and sophistication of farmers.

Ammonia is a successful fertilizer because it has low cost and high nitrogen content. Cost is low because practically all of the other nitrogen fertilizers are made from ammonia, and the raw material must of necessity cost less than the product. The nitrogen content, 82 percent, makes it the most concentrated fertilizer in use.

Liquid fertilizers also came into significant use in the 1950s. Two types are produced, straight nitrogen solutions and mixed liquids. Separate technologies, complicated by the intricacies of solution chemistry, have developed for each.

Nitrogen solutions now hold second place in the nitrogen fertilizer field (in the United States), indicating how rapidly new physical forms of fertilizer have developed; the solid entries in the race have dropped back, with ammonium nitrate in third place and urea in fourth.[1]

The main nitrogen solution is a mixture of urea and ammonium nitrate, used together because the combination

[1] It must be kept in mind, however, that this refers to United States practice, where the pace of innovation has been generally faster than in other parts of the world. Very little ammonia or liquids are used in other countries.

gives much higher solubility (about 32 percent nitrogen) than either alone. Other solutions contain ammonia along with ammonium nitrate and/or urea, to give some of the advantages of both ammonia and solutions.

The mushrooming growth of nitrogen solutions has paralleled that of ammonia. In addition to low cost, the solutions can be handled and applied with less manpower than is required for solid fertilizers. For the future this is a major advantage because farm labor is becoming steadily more scarce and costly.

Mixed liquids have not grown as fast as the straight nitrogen solutions, mainly because the raw materials cost more. The basic operation is reaction of ammonia with phosphoric acid, which is a more expensive raw material than the superphosphate and ammonium phosphate used in making solid mixed fertilizer. Nevertheless, the convenience and low handling cost of the mixed liquids have allowed them to make considerable progress. About 6 percent of the mixed fertilizer in the United States is now applied in liquid form.

Suspension fertilizer is the latest new physical form to appear. Here researchers have tried to get some of the better qualities of both solids and solutions by combining the two, as a suspension of solid particles in a saturated solution. By addition of a gelling agent the suspension is thickened to the point that settling is very slow, like in paint. High nutrient concentration, a major objective in suspensions, can be achieved—typically a 15-15-15—without losing the advantages of the fluid form. Suspension tonnage is not very large as yet, however, because it is so new.

Where and How Big

The major changes since 1950 have altered the fertilizer industry in various ways, including plant location and size. New products have different economics that change the distribution pattern and therefore affect the economics of plant location. Plant size economics are affected also because high concentration of the newer materials makes it feasible to ship farther.

The major development of the 1960s was the great increase in size of ammonia plants. In 1950 a plant unit making 250 tons of ammonia per day was considered a fairly large one; today it would be too small to be economical. Beginning in about 1965 a great wave of expansion swept through the ammonia industry, bringing with it a large number of plants around the world with capacities on the order of 1000 tons per day. More recent units produce 1500 tons and there are plants on the drawing boards designed for 3000 tons per day. Highly automated and designed for an extreme degree of energy conservation, these gigantic plants represent a new level of chemical engineering. In fact, the M. W. Kellogg Company won the Chemical Engineering Award in 1967 for its contribution to the technology of large ammonia plants.

The new ammonia plants are the basic units of the nitrogen industry, for the older, small ones are being shut down rapidly. An important factor in plant location has been the location of raw materials, particularly natural gas which in the United States is located mainly in the Gulf Coast area. Several plants have been built nearer the market areas, however, because natural gas can be transported economically through transcontinental pipe lines (see Fig. 4). In countries that do not have an adequate supply of natural gas, plants are generally located near the source of naphtha, the main alternate to natural gas. If there is no domestic production of naphtha, the ammonia plant may be at the port where the naphtha is imported.

Ammonia is seldom the sole product in nitrogen fertilizer plants. Although the ammonia can be shipped

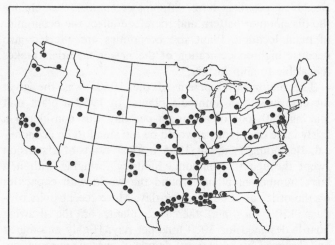

Fig. 4 Ammonia plants in the United States are concentrated in the Gulf Coast areas, close to the source of natural gas, but several plants are located nearer to the main fertilizer market areas.

economically, there are several operating advantages in making products such as ammonium nitrate, urea, and nitrogen solutions at the ammonia plant site. Urea must of necessity be made in conjunction with ammonia, for carbon dioxide, a waste product from ammonia manufacture, is an essential raw material for urea. Shipping of carbon dioxide is impractical.

Hence the typical modern nitrogen fertilizer plant is a complex consisting of ammonia, ammonium nitrate, urea, and nitrogen solution units. The urea production is often carried only to the solution stage and ammonium nitrate mixed with it to make nitrogen solution. There are over thirty such complexes in the United States.

The two superphosphates, ordinary (the older one) and triple, have entirely different economics in regard to plant location and size. The low nutrient concentration of ordinary superphosphate (about 20 percent P_2O_5) makes it costly to ship, so the material is made in small plants—average production of about 35,000 tons per year—located near the market. The high concentration (45 percent P_2O_5 or higher) of triple superphosphate, on the other hand, favors production near the phosphate mines. There are more tons of phosphate ore (30–35 percent P_2O_5) to ship than of triple superphosphate.

There are about 150 ordinary superphosphate plants scattered throughout the United States. Numerous plants are in operation in other parts of the world also, for the material is still the leading phosphate fertilizer on a world basis. In the United States, however, triple superphosphate now supplies the most P_2O_5.

There are only about nineteen triple superphosphate plants in the United States, most of them located in Florida or in the northern Rocky Mountains, near the major phosphate ore deposits. The plants are quite large, on the order of 225,000 tons of product per year.

Potash production is mainly a mining operation located in the desert and mountain areas of the western United States and Canada. In Europe the main production is in Germany and eastern France. Production is very large in the United States plants, an average of about 500,000 tons per year.

The mixed fertilizer industry has become quite complicated in recent years. The main types can be outlined as follows:

1. *Dry mix*. These are produced in the simplest plants, still following the old practice of mechanically mixing ungranulated materials. The practice is declining. There are about five hundred small plants, averaging only about

1500 tons per year each and located mainly in the south-eastern part of the United States. There are still many such plants in other parts of the world.

2. *Ammoniated superphosphate.* Almost half the United States supply of mixed fertilizer is made in plants in which superphosphate is reacted with ammonia and then mixed with other materials. A large proportion of the product is granulated. There are upwards of nine hundred such plants, averaging 10,000 to 20,000 tons per year each.

3. *Ammonium phosphate.* About fifty-five large plants, located mainly in Florida and on the Gulf Coast, average in the neighborhood of 100,000 tons per year each. Ammonium phosphate is the fastest growing mixed fertilizer in the United States, England, and several other areas.

4. *Nitric phosphate.* Only six plants have been built in the United States. Production is mainly by one company and therefore is unreported. In contrast, nitric phosphate is a major fertilizer in continental Europe, produced at the rate of 8,000,000 or more tons per year.

5. *Bulk blends.* Mechanical mixing of high-analysis granular materials (bulk blending) is a rapidly growing practice in the United States but is not important in other countries. There are over 1500 plants, mainly of a local type and averaging 3500 to 4000 tons per year each.

6. *Liquid mixed fertilizer.* The liquid mixes have also grown rapidly in the United States but not in other areas. Over 1000 plants produce about 1100 tons per year each.

The structure of the industry is changing in the United States because of the numerous company mergers taking place in the 1960s. There has been a general effort by the major companies to control the entire sequence, from mining of basic raw materials to sale of final product. Hence large companies have merged and smaller ones have been bought to give a group with the desired diversity of activity—potash and phosphate mining, ammonia and nitrogen fertilizer production, phosphate fertilizer manufacture, fertilizer mixing, and retail distribution. This is a radical change from the older practice, in which the potash, phosphate, nitrogen, and mixed fertilizer industries were quite separate.

The movement of petroleum-based companies into the field has also had a major impact. As such companies already own the raw materials for ammonia, diversification into fertilizer is a logical step.

More change in the industry structure is to be expected as fertilizer production increases to meet the needs of the future. The many plants that must be built in developing countries to help alleviate the growing food shortage will bring in the problems of joint ownership between domestic and foreign investors. Some of the trends now changing the industry in the United States also are active in Europe and Japan, the developed areas, and gradually are coming into effect in other parts of the world. The trend to granulation, greater emphasis on high concentration, and rapid increase in nitrogen fertilizer use are already operating in these areas. Other trends, such as growing use of ammonia as a direct fertilizer and production of fertilizer in liquid or suspension form, no doubt will also move abroad.

What Does It Cost?

The cost of food is one of the most important factors in world economy, particularly in the many countries where hunger is a common thing. With some exceptions, low-cost fertilizer is the most effective single tool in producing food at a price people can afford. The extraordinary success of the fertilizer industry in keeping fertilizer prices at a reasonable level over the past several decades, in a period of rising inflation, has helped immeasurably in feeding the world. In fact, fertilizer cost has actually decreased in the United States over the past fifteen years (see Fig. 5).

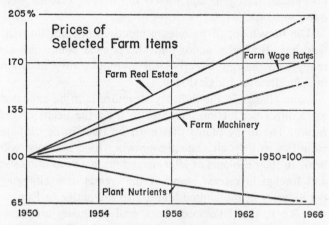

Fig. 5 The cost of food production is made up of several farm inputs. All of these have increased in cost except fertilizer, for which the farmer pays less today than in 1950.

The cost of fertilizer to farmers in the United States, Europe, and Japan ranges from $200 to $250 per ton of nitrogen, $150 to $215 for phosphate ($P_2O_5$), and $65 to $90 for potash ($K_2O$). Although nitrogen appears quite expensive, the others would cost more on the elemental basis—$345 to $495 for phosphorus and $78 to $97 for potassium. Potassium is relatively inexpensive because the mined material requires little processing for use.

Cost in the less-developed countries runs somewhat higher in most instances, because of either high freight cost on imported material or high domestic manufacturing cost.

The good record on fertilizer manufacturing cost has resulted from several factors, among which large plant size is one of the most important. The lower investment and labor requirement per ton of product give a large reduction in the price at which the product must be sold to give a reasonable profit. The large plant has some disadvantage, however, for the product must be distributed over a wider area and shipping cost therefore is higher. But the rapid trend to higher fertilizer use per acre moves the balance back again, reducing the area needed to absorb the large production.

The continuing rise in nutrient content is a major factor in keeping down the cost of handling and shipping. Freight and labor costs have increased so rapidly that the low-analysis fertilizers of the past would be very expensive to distribute today. And beyond delivered cost, high concentration gives a further saving by reducing the farmer's cost of applying to the soil.

The industry has a major economic problem in seasonality of distribution. By this we mean that the farmer uses his fertilizer mainly in the spring (some in the autumn) and does not want to buy it much before he needs it. On the other hand, modern fertilizer plants are much better operated continuously over most of the year. The usual solution is to store the product between fertilizer seasons, but this increases cost because storage buildings or tanks are expensive and a large amount of capital must be tied up in the stored product.

A plus factor is the general trend to handling and using fertilizer in bulk rather than in bags. Before the modern era, almost all fertilizer was bagged because bulk-handling equipment was not available, particularly on the farm. Today bulk handling and application are common in the more advanced countries, thereby reducing cost by several dollars per ton. But in the underdeveloped areas the farmer again must pay more, because the industry is not geared to bulk handling.

CHAPTER 4

Nitrogen

Nitrogen has always had a unique position in fertilizer technology. It is tantalizingly near at hand, 36,000 tons of it in the air over every acre of the earth's surface—in contrast to the limited supplies of phosphate and potash buried deep within the earth in isolated deposits, often in remote and forbidding areas of the world.

But winning nitrogen from the air has proven to be more of a challenge than getting phosphate and potash from under the ground. The aloof nature of the element, refusing to enter into combination with other elements under normal process conditions, has been a major stumbling block to chemists and engineers in their efforts to convert it to a usable form.

There was good reason, then, for reliance on natural nitrogen materials until well into the twentieth century. Of the several types of natural products available, excreta of animals and people was a major one and still remains so, but supplying it is a farm operation rather than part of the commercial fertilizer industry. Manures are too low in nitrogen content and too expensive to gather to have any commercial significance. And as we have seen, modern farming practice cannot depend solely on such a low-analysis and labor-consuming fertilizer even if it is produced on the farm. Only in the backward areas are manures still a major nutrient source. In some of the Oriental countries, for example, the centuries-old practice of gathering night soil (human excreta) and using it as fertilizer continues as the main way of maintaining soil fertility.

Such materials may yet find a place in well-developed

areas, however, for the problem of sewage disposal in large cities grows more troublesome every year. The logical course is to convert it to a physical form usable as fertilizer. Some cities already do this and the practice is likely to spread, but the high cost of shipping the low-grade product to farming areas is a major problem.

Although manure never became a commercial fertilizer of significance, byproducts of meat production were a major nitrogen source in the early part of this century. Tankage (mainly slaughterhouse waste), dried blood, and fish scrap were the main types, reaching the height of their popularity in 1910 to 1920. The fertilizer industry in this period gained the reputation for odor that it has been trying to get away from ever since. Workers in fish scrap plants in those days are said to have used three sets of clothing—one to wear to the front gate of the plant, one to wear through the odorous plant area to their work station, and one to wear at work with the piles of decaying waste.

Plant residues were also a material of importance in the past. Cottonseed meal, castor bean pomace (residue after extraction of oil), peanut hull meal, and soybean meal all contain small percentages of nitrogen and were once fertilizer materials of some note.

Such fertilizers, both from animal and plant sources, are still favored in some areas because of the slow-release nature of the nitrogen, which we shall discuss later. Offsetting this is the relatively high cost. Overall tonnage is quite small.

All this use of plant and animal wastes is merely a continuance of the old practice of returning to the soil that which grew from it. To supplement this limited nitrogen supply, people looked to deposits in the earth. Nitrates have been found scattered over the world but they are so soluble that only in a few areas, such as the dry valley in

Chile, has there been a combination of conditions that preserved the deposit for future use.

Coal is another nitrogen source buried beneath the earth's surface. In eons past, the coal was formed from the great forests and masses of verdure (green vegetation) of prehistoric times; the nitrogen in these plants went into the coal rather than back to the soil by the usual cycle. The nitrogen content is low, about 1 to 2 percent, but when the coal is heated to make coke (rather than burned as fuel), the nitrogen comes out in the form of ammonia gas. Ordinarily this is recovered by contacting the gas with sulfuric acid to make ammonium sulfate. When the use of sodium nitrate from Chile started fading, byproduct ammonium sulfate moved into its place and was the major nitrogen fertilizer in the United States from 1923 to 1947. The amount used today depends on the steel industry— coke is used in making steel and hence coke production, with accompanying recovery of ammonium sulfate, varies with production of steel. Since 1945, byproduct sulfate in the United States has remained fairly constant at about a million tons per year—only about 5 percent of the fertilizer nitrogen used.

Both the nitrate deposits and coal are available to us as fertilizer nitrogen sources because nature accomplished the task of joining nitrogen from the air with other elements to form chemical compounds. Nature uses two methods, one spectacular and the other unobtrusive.

Every lightning flash manufactures nitrate fertilizer. At the extremely high temperature in the lightning bolt, nitrogen combines with oxygen to form nitrogen oxide. Then rain brings it down as nitric acid, and the acid quickly reacts with some alkaline material to form nitrates that dissolve and soak into the soil. It has been estimated that lightning fixes 100,000,000 tons of nitrogen per year, about 8 pounds per acre over the earth's surface.

Nature's other process takes place in the soil rather than in the air. The soil abounds with bacteria that, as part of their life processes, take nitrogen from the air and convert it to organic nitrogen compounds. Some of these, as we have seen, live in nodules attached to the roots of leguminous plants. When the bacteria die the nitrogen becomes part of the supply in the soil—a much less dramatic process than nitrogen oxide formation in the lightning flash but nevertheless an important source of soil nitrogen.

Nitrogen that passes from the air to the soil by these means is taken up by plants, and such plants in the far past formed coal. The nitrate deposits presumably were formed by leaching of soil nitrate into streams feeding lakes that eventually dried up and left their nitrate content as beds of minable material.

Notwithstanding the bounty of nature, the early workers found that coal and natural nitrates were not adequate sources for a large fertilizer nitrogen supply as were the phosphate and potash ores for the other major nutrients. For awhile there was serious consideration of growing legumes as a basic method. Hopkins, as late as 1910, wrote that: "Of course a part of the nitrogen removed in crops may be returned in the manure produced on the farm; and nitrogen may also be bought in the markets in such forms as dried blood, sodium nitrate, and ammonium sulfate. But when we bear in mind that such nitrogen costs from fifteen to twenty cents per pound and that a bushel of corn contains about one pound of nitrogen it will be seen at once that the purchase of nitrogen cannot be considered practicable in general farming.

"Considering all of these facts and the additional facts that there are about 75,000,000 pounds of atmospheric nitrogen resting on every acre of land and that it is possible by bacterial fixation to obtain unlimited quantities of nitrogen from the air for the use of farm crops and at small cost, the inevitable conclusion is that . . . the air is the store from which we must draw. . . ."

It did not turn out that way. Today the farmer can buy fertilizer nitrogen for 10 to 15 cents a pound (less than in Hopkins' time) but the bushel of corn he raises sells for several times the price it brought in those early days. Bacterial fixation seemed simple and foolproof to the early workers. They could not foresee the intensive farming and low-cost chemical fertilizers of the future.

Meanwhile chemists were working hard to find ways to pull the nitrogen from the air. The credit for being the first to succeed, on a plant scale at least, is usually given to Birkeland and Eyde in Norway. Their large-scale tests were preceded, however, by the much earlier work of Henry Cavendish, who in 1766 passed electric sparks through a nitrogen-oxygen mixture and produced nitrogen dioxide. When this was dissolved in water it formed nitric acid. This was the same method that nature uses—the flash of lightning in the thunderstorm. But taming the reaction for practical use seemed for over a hundred years to be as hopeless as harnessing the lightning bolt.

Chemists and engineers persevered. Near the end of the 1800s, Bradley and Lovejoy in the United States and Birkeland and Eyde were near success. In 1902 the Atmospheric Nitrogen Company started up a small plant at Niagara Falls, where plenty of electric power was available, to use the Bradley-Lovejoy method. Dry air was blown through an electric arc to form nitric oxide (NO), the NO was oxidized with oxygen to nitrogen dioxide (NO_2), and the NO_2 was dissolved in water to give nitric acid (HNO_3).

The project turned out to be premature. In 1904 operating troubles forced the company to abandon the operation.

Birkeland and Eyde started up their plant in 1903 and achieved successful commercial operation in 1905. An arc-producing mechanism somewhat different to that of Bradley and Lovejoy was used. The Norwegians also solved the problem of what to do with the product. Since the process gives nitric acid rather than ammonia, materials such as ammonium sulfate, ammonium nitrate, or urea cannot be made. Birkeland and Eyde reacted the acid with limestone (calcium carbonate) to make calcium nitrate, a good fertilizer except for its low nitrogen content and a tendency to get sticky in damp weather.

In the United States another unsuccessful effort at arc fixation was made at Nitrolee, South Carolina, in 1912. Successful operation finally was achieved in a small plant built at La Grande, Washington, in 1917. The plant operated intermittently until 1927 when it was destroyed by fire, which ended the last try at the arc process in the United States.

In Norway operation continued, mainly because of low-cost electric power from the Norwegian rivers, but production finally ceased. Like the lightning flash, the method is very wasteful of energy and cannot compete with the more efficient ammonia synthesis developed later.

But the process refuses to stay dead—the principle of high-temperature reaction of nitrogen and oxygen keeps bobbing up. In the 1950s, Daniels and others developed a furnace-type method in which a bed of pebbles is first heated to high temperature by burning fuel and passing the hot combustion gases through the bed. Then the fuel is cut off and air passed through; at the high temperature a small amount of nitrogen oxide is formed. But the chemistry is such that the nitrogen oxide decomposes if the air is cooled slowly through a range of intermediate temperature that is low enough for the decomposition to occur and high enough to make it happen fast. The solution to this problem is to cool the gas rapidly in another pebble bed to "freeze" the equilibrium and prevent decomposition of the nitrogen oxides. When the cooling bed becomes heated by the gas, flow is reversed and the original cooler becomes the heater.

The Daniels method was tested on a semicommercial scale but was finally abandoned. Although it used a lower cost source of heat than the arc process, and conserved heat better, it did not have enough advantage to compete with low-cost ammonia.

The latest resurgence of the high-temperature nitrogen-oxygen reaction is in connection with MHD power production. MHD is short for *magnetohydrodynamics*, a method for making electric power from combustion heat without raising steam between the heat source and the electric generator. Instead of passing copper wires through a magnetic field as in ordinary generators, power is generated by driving conductive particles through the magnetic field by a jet of hot combustion gas. Nitric oxides are formed as in any combustion process, but with the difference that the MHD operates at very high temperature and therefore generates a relatively large amount of nitrogen oxide. The concentration is possibly high enough to make recovery economically feasible.

The MHD method may have a bright future for power production but the economics of nitrogen oxide recovery are uncertain. There are many practical drawbacks to combining power and fertilizer production. One favorable factor, however, is that low-cost ammonia, now generally available, could be brought in to convert the nitric acid to ammonium nitrate.

At the time the arc process was being developed, other approaches for fixing atmospheric nitrogen were also being studied. Caro and Frank were working in Germany on the calcium cyanamide process. The method was somewhat complicated. First, limestone was burned to quick-lime (CaO), a common process. Then the lime was re-acted with coke at very high temperature in an electric furnace, forming a melt of calcium carbide (CaC_2), a very reactive compound. In a separate operation, air was compressed, liquefied by cooling, and distilled to produce pure nitrogen. The nitrogen and carbide were then com-bined, but not easily, for even though carbide is a highly reactive material a temperature of almost 2000° F. was required to make the inert nitrogen react with it. The product was calcium cyanamide ($CaCN_2$), which is a good fertilizer in itself and is still used to a limited extent. Or the cyanamide could be treated with water under heat and pressure to make ammonia.

The first successful cyanamide plant was built in Italy in 1906, followed by an installation in Canada in 1910. In the United States the first and only effort at cyanamide production was at Muscle Shoals, Alabama, where the U. S. Government built a plant during World War I. But it had nothing to do with fertilizer. The unit was to make cyanamide, but only as an intermediate. The end product was ammonium nitrate made by the steps of treating the cyanamide with water to make ammonia, con-verting part of the ammonia to nitric acid, and reacting the rest of the ammonia with the acid to produce ammonium nitrate.

The ammonium nitrate was needed because it can serve as an explosive for munitions use as well as a fertilizer. The ammonium nitrate was desperately needed at the time because the Germans had cut off the supply of nitrate from Chile, but Armistice Day arrived before the plant was ready to start up. It was never operated except for a two-week test run, and in 1933 was turned over to the newly organized Tennessee Valley Authority and converted to production of other fertilizer materials.

Calcium cyanamide is still made on a limited scale in various parts of the world, but it has little significance as a supplier of fertilizer nitrogen. Frank and Caro deserve credit for their pioneering effort in fixation of nitrogen from the air. They took the wrong route, however, for their process was too complicated for economical production.

Ammonia

If the arc and cyanamide processes had remained the only ones for fixing atmospheric nitrogen, Hopkins might well have been right in his prediction that farmers could never afford nitrogen fertilizer. Fortunately, some of the other early investigators looked in other directions.

Haber and Nernst, beginning about 1900, were working in Germany on combining nitrogen and hydrogen directly to form ammonia. Many others before them had aimed at the same goal but had been frustrated by the unreactive nature of nitrogen. Even at extremely high temperature only a trace of ammonia was formed.

Haber and Nernst were helped immeasurably by the work of Le Chatelier and others who, in the latter half of the nineteenth century, studied equilibria in gas reactions. By equilibrium, we mean that reactants and products reach a steady state in which each is present in a definite concentration in the gas mixture. This involves the principle of *reaction reversibility,* meaning that products can decompose to give the reactants back again if reaction conditions are changed in the proper direction. The situation can be visualized as follows:

$$A + B \rightleftarrows C + D$$

At a given set of reaction conditions (temperature and pressure), A, B, C, and D all exist in the mixture in definite proportions. When A and B are mixed initially, reaction to C and D occurs until the equilibrium concentrations are reached, whereupon the reaction stops. If we start with C and D only, the same thing happens; A and B are formed until the equilibrium concentration is reached.[1]

The German workers found such an equilibrium between nitrogen, hydrogen, and ammonia:

$$N_2 + 3H_2 \rightleftarrows 2NH_3$$

But they also found that under ordinary reaction conditions the equilibrium concentration of ammonia is very low, not enough to make a commercial process possible.

In the reaction, one volume of nitrogen combines with three volumes of hydrogen to give two volumes of ammonia. Le Chatelier had shown earlier that when such a volume decrease occurs, an increase in pressure will shift the equilibrium toward the product. Haber and Nernst used this principle to advantage, working at pressures up to 3000 pounds per square inch to increase the yield of ammonia.

Another of Le Chatelier's principles, however, worked against them. When gas volume decreases during the reaction, an increase in temperature shifts the equilibrium back toward the reactants. Obviously, then, the reaction temperature should be kept low and the pressure high. The trouble with this is that some chemical reactions, including combination of hydrogen and nitrogen to make

[1] For some common reactions, such as hydrogen with oxygen to make water, the equilibrium is so far in the direction of the product that the reactants seem to have disappeared. However, refined methods of analysis will show a few molecules of the reactants still present.

ammonia, are extremely slow at low temperature. A high conversion to product may be attainable at equilibrium, but this is little help if days or even years are required to reach equilibrium. Commercial processes must have a much shorter reaction time—not more than a few hours at most—to be economical.

Thus the unfriendly nature of nitrogen thwarted chemists again. A high temperature was necessary to get the nitrogen molecules excited enough to react, but this pushed the equilibrium the wrong way and offset the beneficial effect of high pressure.

Haber and Nernst tackled this problem by applying to it the relatively new science of catalysis. We shall not try to explore catalysis very far at this point for it is a very complex subject. It is enough to say that a catalyst is a material that, when added to a mixture of reactants, does not enter into the reaction but, by some complex chemical mechanism, makes the reaction go faster than it otherwise would.

Today there are many very important chemical processes, including, for example, "cracking" (breaking-down) of petroleum to make gasoline, that depend on catalysts. In Haber's and Nernst's day there was nothing like this; they were pioneers in applying the new principle to making a sluggish reaction pick up speed.

Haber, Nernst, Mittasch, and their co-workers worked long and hard on the catalyst approach. It was not easy. Over 20,000 experiments were made before a fully acceptable catalyst was developed. Exotic metals such as osmium and uranium were good but too expensive; iron and manganese were more practical but not nearly as effective, in most tests giving less than 1 percent ammonia at equilibrium. Final success came when "promoters," materials such as oxides of aluminum, potassium, and calcium were added to iron. This is the combination still used today.

The new catalyst was quite effective but not enough so to give fast reaction at low temperature. An operating temperature around 1000° F. was necessary, even with the catalyst, to get the very fast conversion rate—a matter of seconds—that was necessary to make the process commercially feasible. At this temperature the ammonia content in the reacted gases was only a few percent even at high pressure. Haber solved this problem by recirculation: the gas mixture was passed through the catalyst, ammonia was condensed (converted to a liquid) and removed by cooling, and the unconverted gases were recirculated back to the catalyst; fresh hydrogen and nitrogen were added after ammonia removal to keep the volume constant. Rapid recirculation gave a high production rate even with low conversion per pass through the catalyst.

This essentially completed the work of the chemists—the chemistry was worked out and the basic process established. But there was still a long way to go before the process could be called a practical commercial operation.

The main trouble was that the high temperatures and pressures needed were new to the chemical engineers of the day. New equipment, materials, and procedures had to be developed, and to this Bosch and his co-workers at the large German chemical firm of Badische Anilin und Soda Fabrik made a mighty contribution. The new technology of high temperature and pressure turned out to be a nightmare of metal corrosion, leaking closures and equipment seals, and danger of explosion. Working out these problems and developing a practical, commercial ammonia process is one of the most brilliant achievements in the history of the chemical industry.

The work was far enough advanced by 1913 that a

commercial plant was started up at Ludwigshafen-Oppau on September 9 of that year. The unit was quite small—only about 38 tons of ammonia per day—in comparison with the giant 1000- to 1500-ton plants of today, but the design principles were much the same as in modern practice (Fig. 6).

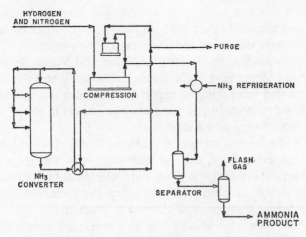

Fig. 6 Modern ammonia synthesis is basically much the same as when Haber and Nernst first developed the process. Nitrogen and hydrogen, compressed to high pressure, are heated to high temperature and passed through a catalyst, where the mixture is partially converted to ammonia. The hot gases leaving the converter give up heat to the incoming gas, are further cooled to condense ammonia, and then are recirculated to the converter.

Great progress was made in the following decades, however, by refining the design. Higher pressure, better ways to cool the catalyst (the reaction gives off a large amount of heat), improved gas flow pattern in the reactor to avoid hot spots, and better gas circulator design—all were steps toward the advanced technology of today. Pressures as high as 15,000 pounds per square inch are now used, although about 4500 pounds is more common. Numerous converter designs have been developed, each named after the developer. Catalysts now last much longer because improved design has reduced damage from local overheating.

All this has to do with converting a carefully proportioned mixture of pure nitrogen and hydrogen to ammonia. But where do we get the nitrogen and hydrogen?

Nitrogen was no problem to Haber and Nernst. It was present everywhere in the air and, although it was the element they were trying to capture for fertilizer use, actually it could be brought into the ammonia process in almost an incidental way, as we shall see.

Hydrogen was more of a problem. It was also available almost everywhere, tied up with oxygen in the form of water, but converting it to the pure, elemental form needed was almost as much a challenge as the main objective, converting hydrogen and nitrogen to ammonia.

Bosch took the lead in this. It was already known that carbon would react with water at high temperature to give hydrogen.

$$C + H_2O \longrightarrow H_2 + CO$$

It was a long way from the laboratory to the plant, however, and years elapsed before Bosch and his co-workers had a practical process. For one thing, coal, the cheapest source of carbon, had so much volatile tars in it that equipment quickly became clogged. Coke, which is coal from which the volatile matter has been boiled out, worked much better.

But an even worse problem was that the reaction is

endothermic (requiring heat). The metals of the day were not up to the duty of transferring heat through tube or furnace walls at the high reaction temperature involved.

The early workers solved this problem by supplying heat directly to the gas stream; air to burn part of the coal was added along with the steam.

$$2C + H_2O + O_2 \longrightarrow H_2 + CO + CO_2$$

Heat from the burning coal supplied the heat soaked up by the carbon-water reaction.

Now another problem entered. Air contains over three times as much nitrogen as oxygen, so when enough air was used to generate the needed reaction heat there was far more nitrogen than needed to make ammonia. The excess nitrogen could not be left in the gas because it would accumulate in the ammonia synthesis loop.

The ingenuity of the early engineers was equal to this task also. They made the operation a cyclic one; that is, they blew air alone through the coke bed to heat it to a high temperature, about 1100° F. Then the air was cut off and the steam turned on until the bed cooled to about 900°, after which the cycle was repeated. During the steam "blow" and part of the air "blow" the gas was passed to the ammonia plant. The gas valve was then turned to vent the unwanted nitrogen from the rest of the air blow to the stack.

Bosch then had a mixture of hydrogen, nitrogen, carbon monoxide (CO), and carbon dioxide (CO$_2$). The carbon oxides had to be removed because they were poisonous to the newly developed ammonia catalyst; that is, they ruined its effectiveness when present in the gas.

But the carbon monoxide still had some chemical potential left in it since it was only half way between carbon and carbon dioxide. It was known—again, a laboratory reaction—that carbon monoxide would react with water.

$$CO + H_2O \longrightarrow H_2 + CO_2$$

But, like ammonia synthesis, the equilibrium was pushed the wrong way by high temperature and the reaction was slow at low temperature.

So back to catalyst development. This time iron oxide, with certain promoters, turned out to be the most practical combination. Wild, of BASF, developed the catalyst in 1915 and determined the best operating conditions.

Now the German workers had hydrogen, nitrogen, and carbon dioxide. Removal of the carbon dioxide was relatively easy because it is soluble in water and hydrogen and nitrogen are not—at least to any significant extent. By passing the gas upward through a "scrubbing" (gas absorption) tower, under pressure and countercurrent to water spraying or trickling down, they effectively removed the carbon dioxide.

But the job was not yet done. Although the reaction with water had removed most of the carbon monoxide from the gas, the equilibrium was not good enough to get all of it out and the residue was too high for the health of the ammonia catalyst.

Another gas absorption (scrubbing) operation was therefore introduced, this time a copper formate liquor that had to be cooled to low temperature (about 32° F.) to be effective. This reduced the carbon oxides in the gas to a few parts per million, low enough to avoid poisoning of the ammonia catalyst.

Thus the long and arduous development of the complicated ammonia process was completed. It demanded the best of the chemists and engineers of the day, and is certainly one of the outstanding chemical engineering achievements of all time. Actually it was more than development of an ammonia process, for the new construction materials, the development of high temperature and pressure techniques, and the new catalyst technology were soon applied in other fields as well. Ammonia technology became a foundation for development of many other important chemical processes.

In modern times coke is seldom used as a raw material for ammonia. It is expensive, and the cyclic "blow" process is cumbersome by modern standards. Natural gas or naphtha (a petroleum fraction), which are much cheaper and easier to use, are reacted with steam in today's plants by a process that gives hydrogen at low cost.

It is important to note that the significant raw material for nitrogen fertilizer production is not air, the source of the nitrogen. Neither is it the water that supplies hydrogen, for water is cheap. The only material involved that costs very much is the natural gas or naphtha used to break up the water molecules in making hydrogen—and carbon, the important reactant in these materials, does not even end up in the product.

This devious route to nitrogen fertilizer is quite important in modern times because it makes the natural carbonaceous materials—natural gas, petroleum, and coal—the basic raw materials. We have vast reserves of these so the foreseeable future of fertilizer nitrogen production is assured. And when, sometime far in the future, we must take another direction, nuclear or solar energy will be a good alternate. The electricity made from these energy sources can be used to break water down directly to hydrogen and oxygen.

Natural gas is such an economical raw material for ammonia that countries possessing it have a considerable advantage in producing nitrogen fertilizer. Many countries, however, have no gas. In recent years most of these have turned to naphtha, a liquid material that can be imported economically by tank ship.

The process is the same for either natural gas or naphtha. Water (in the form of steam) is mixed with the natural gas or naphtha (vaporized by preheating) and the mixture heated to very high temperature. But here the situation is reversed as compared to ammonia synthesis; one volume of steam plus one of natural gas makes four volumes of hydrogen plus one of carbon monoxide. Hence Le Chatelier's principle gives us better conversion at low pressure and high temperature. Fortunately, the equilibrium is much better than for the ammonia reaction. By using very high temperature (about 1600° F.) the reaction can be pushed almost to completion, leaving very little unconverted natural gas or naphtha in the product gas mixture. If this were not possible we would be in trouble, for recycling the gases after product removal would not be practical. Unlike ammonia, hydrogen cannot be condensed economically and removed as a liquid from the unreacted gases.

Even at the high temperature the reaction is too slow for economical process operation. So we turn again to a catalyst, this time nickel. The catalyst is carried in tubes suspended in a furnace equipped with gas or oil burners; the steam-gas mixture passes through the tubes and the burners outside drive enough heat through the tube walls to keep the endothermic reaction going.

The reaction is not completed in the catalyst tubes. Air is injected into the gas leaving the catalyst, to raise the temperature by burning out part of the hydrogen, and the gas is then passed through a mass of catalyst to finish the conversion. Only enough air is used, of course, to furnish the nitrogen needed for ammonia synthesis.

As to other parts of the process, the carbon monoxide–steam reaction step is still much the same as in the early days. Better absorbents than water have been developed for carbon dioxide removal, however, and the old copper liquor method for removing residual carbon monoxide is also obsolete. In modern plants the gas passes through a catalyst that causes the carbon monoxide to react with hydrogen, forming methane (CH_4) and water. The methane can be left in the gas without harming the ammonia catalyst and the water is removed by the compressors in raising the gas to synthesis pressure.

Hence the modern ammonia process has four catalytic steps, each requiring a different catalyst. Without catalysis Hopkins' argument that nitrogen fertilizers cost too much might well be true today.

Instead we have giant ammonia plants whose catalytic converters turn out ammonia at amazingly low cost, on the order of $15 to $20 per ton. As a result the farmer gets nitrogen fertilizers at lower cost than in the past even though costs generally have gone up. For developing countries, who generally lack "hard money," this is particularly important. The great strides in ammonia technology in the past decade or so have been a major contribution to feeding the world.

The story of ammonia would not be complete without telling about its beginning as a fertilizer. In the early 1930s agricultural workers conceived the idea of putting ammonia in irrigation water as an inexpensive way of applying fertilizer. It worked well, for the ammonia was so diluted by the water that it soaked into the soil with little vapor loss. Later someone had the bold idea that water might not be necessary, that the ammonia could be injected directly into the soil. This was a radical concept, for ammonia is a liquid only when under high pressure, over 150 pounds per square inch at summer temperature; if a valve on top of a tank is opened, the liquid boils furiously and ammonia gas rushes out. To use such a liquid as a fertilizer seemed very dubious.

The early experimenters tried it, however, and it worked quite well. They found that if the ammonia was injected about 6 inches under the soil surface and covered up quickly there was little or no loss. The fine soil particles absorbed the gas rapidly and held it until normal conversion to nonvolatile nitrate took place.

Equipment for injecting the ammonia was also a problem. Opening the soil to the proper depth, injecting the ammonia, and closing the opening, all without using a large amount of power, was difficult. The problem was solved by using a curved injection "knife"; the sharp leading edge slides easily through the soil and a tube fastened to the back of the knife delivers the ammonia to the bottom of the furrow where it vaporizes instantaneously and is absorbed. A follower pushes soil into the narrow furrow and prevents loss of the ammonia gas.

After the first tests, farmers gradually took up the new way of applying fertilizer; with typical caution they did not rush into it. The economic advantage was a powerful persuader, however, because using the ammonia directly eliminated the cost of converting it to solid fertilizers like ammonium sulfate and ammonium nitrate. The saving was so great that ammonia could be applied on large farms such as in the Mississippi Delta area for 7.5 cents per pound of nitrogen (total cost in the soil) as compared with about 13 cents for ammonium nitrate.

One other thing remained to be developed before ammonia could become a general fertilizer. Solid fertilizer such as ammonium nitrate can be stored in existing buildings without any great difficulty but ammonia cannot. Tank "farms" had to be built and a general distribution system set up, designed to take care of the difficult handling and storage properties of the new material. This was done;

today there is a well-organized ammonia distribution system spread over the United States, capable of quickly supplying the great demand by farmers at the beginning of each spring planting season.

American farmers have taken full advantage of ammonia's low cost, even though it is more difficult to handle. In 1950 less than 100,000 tons of fertilizer nitrogen was applied as ammonia in the United States; in 1967, the figure was about 2,000,000 tons, practically as much as for all other nitrogen fertilizers combined.

The rapid trend to using ammonia as a fertilizer in the United States has not been repeated in other parts of the world. There the older fertilizers such as ammonium sulfate and ammonium nitrate are still favored. Several things contribute to this: smaller farms, less able to bear the large investment in pressure tanks and application equipment; lower technical level among farmers and less ability to master handling and application techniques; and slowness in developing and installing the costly distribution systems required. But the pattern is changing; in Denmark, for example, a fair amount of ammonia use has grown up in the past few years. Eventually ammonia should become the leading nitrogen fertilizer throughout the world as well as in the United States; the economic push is there but it will take time to change farmer attitudes and capabilities.

Ammonium Sulfate

Except for low nutrient content (21 percent nitrogen), ammonium sulfate is a very good fertilizer; it stores well (little trouble from caking), has little sensitivity to heat and shock, and can be made cheaply in many situations where byproducts are involved.

It is also a very old fertilizer. Byproduct ammonium sulfate was made in England as early as 1840, about the same time that superphosphate appeared on the scene. In the

United States the material appeared sometime later, about 1893.

The byproduct label has been associated with ammonium sulfate all through its history, mainly in connection with coke production but also in other processes, as we shall see. Coke is required in all countries, because steel is a basic, essential material and coke plays a major role in its production. The coke is made in a fairly simple process—coal is heated to boil out the volatile impurities that would interfere in smelting and the many other operations in which coke is used. The gas that comes off the coal during coking is a mixture of ammonia, carbon dioxide, hydrogen, methane, steam, and small drops of tar. Recovering values from it is not easy. A convenient way of catching the ammonia is by reaction with sulfuric acid; the two have a great affinity for each other. After some purification, the water is evaporated and ammonium sulfate crystallizes out.

Manufacture of caprolactam, the main intermediate in production of nylon, is another source of byproduct ammonium sulfate. Considerably more ammonium sulfate is made than caprolactam, about a 4.5:1 ratio, so ammonium sulfate production is significant even though caprolactam is a relatively low-tonnage product.

Another source is byproduct gypsum (calcium sulfate) from production of phosphoric acid. Here also 4 or 5 tons of gypsum are made per ton of acid (P_2O_5 basis) so the useless gypsum piles up. Enterprising engineers in Germany, in the 1920s, worked out a method of putting the waste material to some use, by reacting it with ammonia and carbon dioxide to make ammonium sulfate and calcium carbonate. This ends up with another byproduct, the calcium carbonate, in an amount about as large as the original gypsum, but the carbonate is useful as a liming agent for the soil.

The gypsum conversion method is unique in that the sulfate, in effect, is used twice—first (as sulfuric acid) in dissolving phosphate ore and second in making ammonium sulfate. Few processes accomplish such a double use of a main reactant.

Byproduct sulfuric acid often figures in ammonium sulfate production. Petroleum refineries, petrochemical plants, soap factories, and some metallurgical processes use sulfuric acid in such a way that it comes out with part or all its acid value intact but with a heavy load of impurities picked up along the way. This "gunk" is often a disposal headache, too dirty to give away and too acid to drain away to rivers. Here the fertilizer industry can step in, because fertilizers do not have to be pure and can use the waste acid in production of ammonium sulfate and other fertilizers.

Ammonium sulfate is not always made from byproduct materials. When no byproducts are available, "virgin" ammonia and acid are often used; in fact, this type of production accounted for 238,000 tons in 1963. This is an expensive way to make fertilizer, however, for all the sulfuric acid does is convert ammonia to a solid form. The acid supplies no nutrient as nitric acid does in making ammonium nitrate or phosphoric acid in production of ammonium phosphate. The main reason for making ammonium sulfate this way is that sulfuric acid has been cheap in the past—but this is a situation that is passing, for sulfuric acid, as we shall see later, is becoming an expensive acid because of the world sulfur shortage.

Ammonium nitrate and urea are gradually pushing ammonium sulfate into the background. The ammonium sulfate "reign" in the United States was from 1923, when it took over from sodium nitrate, to 1947 when ammonium nitrate moved into first place (to be displaced a decade later by ammonia). On the world basis ammonium sulfate held out somewhat longer, until 1959. Production is still increasing but the more concentrated materials are growing faster.

Ammonium Nitrate

The fact that ammonium nitrate is the leading nitrogen fertilizer of the world is a major tribute to the chemists and engineers who put it there, for the compound has such major shortcomings that it is a most unlikely candidate for high fertilizer position.

For one thing, the hygroscopicity is quite high, meaning that the material absorbs moisture from the atmosphere rapidly and therefore becomes sticky—a condition that is not conducive to flow from a fertilizer distributor. The major problem, though, as we have discussed earlier, is that in storage the moisture absorbed on the particles dissolves some ammonium nitrate which, when the temperature drops, crystallizes out and cements particles together. This caking is one of the major problems with high concentration products such as ammonium nitrate; the high nitrogen content is associated chemically with high solubility and hence with a great thirst for atmospheric moisture. To get the high nutrient content essential to offset high handling and shipping costs, the hygroscopicity and caking problems must be accepted.

In the early days of ammonium nitrate production, caking was such a problem that the term "tombstone fertilizer" was sometimes applied to it. Bags of nitrate caked so hard that they did somewhat resemble tombstones. Much progress has been made since then in improving the physical condition. Numerous conditioning agents have been developed that when coated onto the particle surface protect it from moisture and delay caking. The effect is not one of completely preventing moisture absorption, which would be very difficult, but rather of controlling the crystallization to reduce caking. Finely ground clay, for example, holds the particles a slight distance apart and thus makes it harder for the crystal bridges to form.

Clays are the most widely used conditioners. Organic surface-active agents are also helpful, and many other types have been used. Drying to very low moisture content before storage is important, and making the particles porous, by proper control of granule formation, helps because the particle acts something like a sponge by sucking much of the absorbed moisture into the particle interior where it cannot take part in building crystal bridges.

Aside from caking, ammonium nitrate has some troublesome properties all its own. One of these comes from its crystal nature. The compound has five different crystal forms, each of which is stable over a certain range of temperature. Unfortunately, form IV changes to form III at about 90° F., and, even worse, form III needs more room so the crystals expand when they go through the transition. Then when night comes, or the weather turns cool, they shrink back to form IV. The particles cannot stand much of this so they soon fall apart. The problem has been particularly bad in shipping bulk ammonium nitrate in railroad hopper cars during the summer; the hot sun on the side of the car heats the material through the 90° F. transition and the night brings the temperature back down again. The cure for crystal transition is to add a small amount of a magnesium or potassium compound. These materials raise the transition temperature to a level not encountered under ordinary weather conditions.

Probably the most noted bad feature of ammonium nitrate has to do with the unsociable nature of elemental nitrogen that we dealt with in an earlier chapter. The early workers soon learned that nitrogen reacts with other elements and compounds very grudgingly; later investigators found that the opposite is just as true. When ammonium nitrate is subjected to sufficient shock it decomposes—and the nitrogen returns to its elemental form with explosive velocity. Throughout its history ammonium nitrate has travelled in the shadow of its dual personality—an effective plant food when undisturbed but a violent explosive when some force releases the pent-up inclination of the nitrogen to be free.

Some of the early work was aimed at exploiting the unstable nature of the material. At Notodden, Norway, in the years before World War I, dilute solutions of nitric acid and ammonia were mixed and ammonium nitrate crystallized out. The process was developed in time for the war, and ammonium nitrate became a major military explosive. After the war, the fertilizer industry turned its attention to nitrate because of its obvious good points. There was concern, of course, about using an explosive as a fertilizer but there appeared to be little or no danger under ordinary handling conditions. To make sure, other materials such as calcium carbonate or ammonium sulfate were mixed with the nitrate, a proven way of reducing sensitivity. Nevertheless, trouble came. In Oppau, Germany, on September 21, 1921, there occurred one of the major tragedies in the history of fertilizer production. A large mass of ammonium nitrate mixed with ammonium sulfate, supposedly a safe material, exploded. The destruction was tremendous; 586 people were killed, 1952 were injured, and 2138 buildings were destroyed. Many theories have been advanced as to the cause of the explosion, but to this day it is still not clear why, after years of uneventful production of the material, it should suddenly become triggered and the vast energy released.

Much experimental work was done to determine what combinations of factors cause detonation and how to avoid them. This was not easy, because ammonium nitrate is so insensitive that the experimenters were hard put to make it explode for their tests. It was easy to get it to burn, for the oxygen required for combustion is carried within the molecule along with the nitrogen and hydrogen that oxidize during burning. But it was soon found that conditions which cause burning very seldom cause detonation; the chemistries of the two reactions are entirely different.

Ammonium nitrate returned to its role as a munition in World War II. In the United States several ammonium nitrate plants, with associated ammonia and nitric acid units, were built to supply the needs of war. Before the war was over, however, military researchers had developed explosives more powerful and easier to use than ammonium nitrate, and plants were built to produce them. At the same time a great need for fertilizer had developed because the war had interfered with normal supplies. So ammonium nitrate changed back from Hyde to Jekyll and became a much needed fertilizer, which is about as close to beating the sword into a plowshare as history recounts.

At the time, ammonium nitrate was not a familiar material to farmers in the United States; there had been some previous use but it was quite small. But they needed the fertilizer badly so they accepted it, even though some of the early material caked so extremely that the bag of nitrate became one large, hundred-pound lump. Industry and government researchers attacked this problem vigorously and soon developed a conditioning treatment—coating with a mixture of petrolatum, rosin, and paraffin—that prevented the caking.

After the war, industry bought up the nitrate plants and operated them to supply the demand that had developed among farmers. Ammonium nitrate rapidly became a major fertilizer. There was little or no mixing with other materials to reduce the danger of explosion, although this was still the standard practice in Europe. In the United States, the longer shipping distances and generally higher labor cost made it quite costly to mix anything with the ammonium nitrate that would reduce the nutrient content.

Then in 1947 came another of the unfortunate accidents that have clouded the history of ammonium nitrate. In Texas City, Texas, two ships—the S.S. *Grandcamp* and the S.S. *High Flyer*—were in port loaded with ammonium nitrate fertilizer. One of them caught fire, from some unknown cause. The captain, accustomed to fighting shipboard fires of the normal type, battened down the hatches —about the worst thing he could have done because it allowed heat and pressure to develop below decks. Shutting off oxygen from the fire did not help as it normally would because the ammonium nitrate carried its own oxygen. In a few hours the ship exploded, and the explosion set off the other ship loaded with ammonium nitrate. Devastation in the harbor and the nearby city was enormous; over 450 people lost their lives and a good part of the city was destroyed.

Industry and government quickly took steps to improve ammonium nitrate safety. Research showed that the organic conditioner used was a sensitizer so its use was abandoned; the clays now generally used took its place. The Coast Guard set up handling and loading regulations designed to prevent the combination of conditions that developed at Texas City, ocean shipping of straight ammonium nitrate was generally abandoned, and new safety procedures were adopted throughout the industry.

For over twenty years now there has been no major trouble with ammonium nitrate. Research has shown that the mass involved is a major factor; small and medium quantities are very difficult to detonate (unless set off by another explosion), but in very large masses such as those that exploded at Oppau and Texas City, thermal decomposition in the interior can release energy that builds up in intensity, because the large mass holds it in and keeps it from dissipating, until finally it triggers detonation, a reaction that develops tremendous energy and travels faster than the speed of sound.

There are still ammonium nitrate fires and explosions but they are accidents such as may occur with many common chemical materials, including gasoline. It has been well demonstrated that with adequate precautions there is no hazard in handling and shipping. Today the double nature of the material has been controlled and put to good use. Mixed with fuel oil to increase detonation sensitivity, ammonium nitrate serves as an effective and economical industrial explosive. Coated with clay or other conditioners to reduce sensitivity, it is an effective and economical fertilizer, in fact, the major nitrogen fertilizer of the world.

Making ammonium nitrate is a relatively simple procedure, which is one of the reasons it is an economical fertilizer. We merely mix ammonia with nitric acid, evaporate the water that came in with the acid, and form the ammonium nitrate into small pellets. The reaction of the ammonia and acid is very rapid and develops a large amount of heat, so if we manage the system right this heat will evaporate the water. In modern plants this is done, and little outside heat has to be supplied.

Then, with all the water out, we have molten ammonium nitrate at an elevated temperature. How can the hot melt be converted to the fertilizer pellets we want? The principal method for doing this, used in the majority of plants, is not new at all—at least not in principle. The early pioneers had a manufacturing problem of great importance to them; they needed shot to load their guns and the shot had to be perfectly round if they were to get the accuracy that their lives sometimes depended on. Lacking manufacturing equipment, they solved the problem quite simply by melting lead, pouring it through a perforated container to form drops, and letting the drops fall far enough through the air to harden them during the fall. This is exactly the way ammonium nitrate melt is handled today; the old "shot tower" has become the modern "prilling tower."

After the prills are formed, we must make sure that they are as dry as possible; the drier the better to reduce caking later on. In the usual process, a little water remains in the melt fed to the prilling tower, and this must be removed by passing the prills through large dryers. Then we cool the prills, shake them with clay, and the job is done. The very fine clay particles stick to the prills well enough that 1 or 2 percent can be applied without using a sticking agent.

This is the way that straight ammonium nitrate, unmixed with anything else, is made. But as we have mentioned earlier, much of the ammonium nitrate is mixed with some other material before it reaches the farmer. These mixes are mainly made by entirely different methods, most of which will be described later when we discuss multinutrient fertilizers. We must not forget, however, that nitrogen solutions are the second most important nitrogen fertilizer in the United States and that most of them contain ammonium nitrate—usually mixed with urea. Here we do not go through the prilling process, but merely react ammonia with nitric acid, cool, and mix with urea solution. This costs less than going through the prilling procedure so the solutions ordinarily are less expensive than solid nitrogen fertilizers.

What of ammonium nitrate today? With all its problems, we may well ask how it is faring.

For the last five years reported by FAO (Food and Agricultural Organization, a branch of the United Nations), ammonium nitrate held steady at 28 to 29 percent of world fertilizer nitrogen. The high concentration (33.5 percent nitrogen) and low production cost keep it in top position but it has stopped gaining (as it did for many years) because more promising materials are on the horizon. Nevertheless, it should retain its standing as the world's leading nitrogen fertilizer for many years.

Urea

In 1773 a chemist named Rouelle found that he could isolate about 20 grams of a white crystalline substance from a liter of urine; he named it urea, after urine. Some years later the chemical structure was found to be NH_2-CO-NH_2. But it was in 1828 that urea really caught the attention of chemists, for it was in that year Wöhler prepared urea from ammonium cyanate, an inorganic compound.

$$NH_4CNO \xrightarrow{\text{heat}} NH_2CONH_2$$
$$\text{ammonium cyanate} \qquad \text{urea}$$

The excitement came from the fact that this was the first time anyone had ever made an organic compound in the laboratory. (Organic compounds were defined as those made by nature in living processes.) Some regard Wöhler's work as the beginning of synthetic organic chemistry. Today, of course, we manufacture hundreds of organic compounds without recourse to living processes.

But urea was not to remain merely a laboratory curiosity marking the beginning of a new chemical era. In 1868 Basarow learned how to make it from ammonia and carbon dioxide, which, because of the simple raw materials, brought it into consideration as a product that might be made economically on a large scale.

As usual, however, the way was not easy. Like nitrogen and hydrogen in ammonia production, the ammonia and carbon dioxide refuse to react completely like ammonia and nitric acid do in manufacturing of ammonium nitrate. This was an old problem to Bosch, in Germany, who as we have seen earlier fought the same type of battle in developing ammonia synthesis. So after the ammonia development was well along the way, he started on urea.

The problem was somewhat different. Raw materials were readily available, in contrast to the trouble Bosch had had in getting pure nitrogen and hydrogen for ammonia, for the ammonia plant supplied both ammonia and carbon dioxide in pure form. In fact, the carbon dioxide that was formerly discarded after removal from the nitrogen-hydrogen mixture now became a valuable raw material for urea.

But then the troubles began. Bosch and the other workers had been lucky in synthesis gas production and in ammonia synthesis because these processes, even though carried out at very high temperature, can be operated for years in ordinary steel without any great damage to equipment. Urea was different. The ammonia-carbon dioxide mixture was so corrosive that it would eat through a reactor in a short time. In fact, it chewed up equipment so fast that the product was colored red with dissolved iron. The corrosion problem was worse than it might have been because, like ammonia, high pressure and temperature promoted conversion. These conditions, which also promote corrosion, made it impossible to use ordinary steel.

What to do? Obviously, use something other than steel. Some of the early developers went so far as to use silver, not for the entire reactor but as a lining to keep the urea away from the steel. Lead was also found suitable and soon became widely used.

Today silver is never used and lead very seldom; both are too expensive. Surprisingly, steel is again the preferred material. Somewhere along the way someone learned that a small amount of oxygen in the gas mixture will form an oxide film on the steel and protect it. So today, in practically all urea plants, a little air is fed into the carbon dioxide before it enters the reactor. The effect is somewhat remarkable because oxygen normally aggravates corrosion rather than reducing it. Of such is chemical process progress made.

The air injection helped tremendously but not enough to allow the use of ordinary steel. The stainless type (steel containing some chromium and nickel), however, gives good service. Even with this there is a temperature limitation, about 380° F. It would be good to go higher to get faster conversion and this may be possible with some of the newer metals—titanium or zirconium, for example.

Curing corrosion was only the first step. The next obstacle was the incomplete reaction—what to do with the unreacted ammonia and carbon dioxide. Again, the problem was quite different from the incomplete reaction in ammonia synthesis, where the gases could merely be chased around a high-pressure loop, making ammonia at one point, cooling to condense it out at another, and adding makeup gas at a third. In urea synthesis, unfortunately, water is a reaction product as well as urea:

$$2NH_3 + CO_2 \longrightarrow NH_2CONH_2 + H_2O$$

At the high pressure in the reactor, the water condenses and dissolves everything—the product is a solution containing the urea and most of the unreacted ammonia and carbon dioxide. The only way to get the ammonia and carbon dioxide out is to release the pressure; then, if the solution is hot enough, the gases bubble out readily.

Recycling the ammonia and carbon dioxide seems simple enough—merely compress them back to reactor pressure and inject them along with fresh makeup gas into the reactor. This was what Bosch did, but it did not work very well. Compressors normally go up in pressure a step at a time; there is cooling between stages to reduce power requirement and compressor size. When Bosch tried cooling between stages, ammonium carbamate, an intermediate compound in urea synthesis, condensed in the compressor.

$$2NH_3 + CO_2 \longrightarrow NH_2CO_2NH_4$$

Moreover, since each cylinder was acting like a miniature urea reactor, corrosion was severe. Bosch eliminated the cooling to get around carbamate formation, but this made power requirement high and did not help corrosion. The method was eventually abandoned because of these troubles.

So where to go from this? Here was a good product, an efficient, highly concentrated fertilizer and a chemical useful in many other fields, but there was no economical way to produce it. The corrosive mixture of ammonia and carbon dioxide had to be recycled and there was no good way to do it.

Why not recycle as a solution in water so that pumps rather than gas compressors could be used? This was tried and with some success, but the pumps of the day were not very efficient at pumping such a corrosive solution against the very high pressure. So the developers looked for other methods.

Then how about separating the ammonia and carbon dioxide and recycling them separately, which would avoid both carbamate deposition and corrosion? A good idea— processes were developed for separating the gases and several plants were built in which this principle was used.

The gas separation method works well but investment is somewhat high and it is less flexible than recycling without separation. As an alternate, urea process engineers looked at water recycling again. During the course of the several decades since the method was first tested, pump design and operation had improved, to the extent that newer designs might be able to pump corrosive solution against high pressure. So water recycling was tried again and, with a few new gimmicks, it worked quite well. Today the method is being used in most of the new plants built.

So patience and good engineering finally conquered the recycle problem. With this out of the way, the process was further refined until the cost of making urea was no higher than for producing ammonium nitrate; urea requires expensive pressure equipment and costly recycling but these are offset by the nitric acid plant cost in making ammonium nitrate.

With the new processing techniques, urea thrived. We noted earlier that ammonium nitrate, the main nitrogen fertilizer, barely held its own, at 27 to 28 percent of total fertilizer nitrogen, over the last five years reported (1960–65). In contrast, urea went from 6 percent to 11 percent in the same period. With its high nitrogen content (46 percent nitrogen), use of urea will quite likely continue along this trend, in which case it will become the leader in the early 1980s.

We left the production discussion at the point where unreacted ammonia and carbon dioxide were boiled out of the urea solution. Much of this solution is used as is in making liquid fertilizers such as the urea-ammonium nitrate solution described earlier, but, as in ammonium nitrate production, part is converted to a solid product. Since both ammonium nitrate and urea have low melting points, they can be finished in the same way—by evaporating the water and prilling the melt.

But, again like ammonium nitrate, urea has some troublesome problems. The nitrate decomposes violently under heavy shock; urea, in contrast, decomposes slowly and gently under processing conditions that would have no effect on ammonium nitrate at all. The production superintendent is the main figure in this problem. If he were making ammonium nitrate, he would have little difficulty —because detonation (explosion) is more of a problem in storing and shipping than in production—but in the urea plant decomposition starts as soon as the urea leaves the reactor and is freed from unreacted ammonia. All that the production people can do is keep the temperature as low as possible and rush the urea through the plant with minimum delay so that it can be cooled down to stop the decomposition. With good operation, decomposition can be held to less than 0.5 percent.

The decomposition is more serious than the 0.5 percent sounds, for the product formed is biuret:

$$2NH_2CONH_2 \xrightarrow{\text{heat}} NH_2CONHCONH_2 + NH_3$$

$$\text{urea} \qquad\qquad\qquad \text{biuret} \qquad \text{ammonia}$$

The biuret, unfortunately, is a fair herbicide for some plants (particularly citrus) if present in high enough concentration. Under most situations, however, there is very little chance of damage by the small amount of biuret formed in normal plant operation.

Urea's instability follows it to the soil, but here the decomposition is not to biuret but back to ammonia and carbon dioxide. Urea scattered on the soil surface, particularly where plants are growing and when the weather is hot, can decompose and lose a considerable amount of ammonia to the air before rain comes and washes it into the soil. The reason that plants (or plant residues) promote decomposition is that they contain an enzyme called urease that acts as a catalyst to the decomposition reaction. So nature in the end, with its own catalyst, undoes what man did with his catalysts in forming the ammonia from which the urea was made. But the damage can be avoided merely by covering the urea with soil so that any ammonia lost will be absorbed by the soil rather than lost to the air.

Slow-Release Nitrogen

The nitrogen fertilizers we have been talking about—ammonium sulfate, ammonium nitrate, and urea—are, in the main, good ones, and without them there would be far less food in the world. But they all have one major drawback that has been the despair of agronomists throughout modern fertilizer history. They dissolve too fast when placed in the soil.

Consider a granule of ammonium nitrate. You can get a bag of such granules at most any farm store, and when you open the bag there are thousands of small, dry, flowable spheres. But put one of them outside on a dry surface. In a few minutes it will begin to grow damp, before long it begins to collapse as moisture absorbed from the air begins to dissolve it, and finally there is only a damp spot to show where the ammonium nitrate had been.

It is no wonder, then, that soluble nitrogen fertilizers placed in or on the soil dissolve immediately. You may ask why this would worry the agronomists, since, as we have said earlier, fertilizers must dissolve before the plant can use them. The trouble is that if they dissolve too early, before the plant is ready for them, they may never get to the plant at all.

In a very hard rain as much as 3 or 4 inches of rain may fall in the course of an hour or so. The soil cannot absorb all of this, so much of the water flows along the surface, off into water courses. But a good portion, particularly in well-drained soils, goes on through the top layers of the soil and into the subsoil that the plow never touches; in periods of heavy rainfall this type of flow is shown by springs that come to life or increase their output.

The downward flow of water takes the dissolved nitrogen fertilizer with it—a process called "leaching"—and the farmer may be left without enough nitrogen for his crop. Much the same thing happens when the surface water floods across the soil surface; the water dissolves and takes with it any surface-applied fertilizer and carries it into the rivers and lakes where it fulfills its function of supplying plant nutrient but in a very undesirable way, by making aquatic plants grow faster, which irritates boatmen, swimmers, and others who want clear, uncluttered water for recreational use.

The rapid dissolving in the soil is bad in other ways. For one thing, plants are quite delicate when they first emerge from the seed, and do best if exposed only to the gentle nurture of the natural soil solution. They need to be larger and stronger before they can take the strong food supplied by highly concentrated fertilizers. So if a pellet of nitrogen fertilizer happens to be close to a seed, the strong solution that forms quickly as the pellet dissolves is likely to kill the plant as it breaks the seed case.

And as we have seen earlier, plants, like people, eat too much if they have plenty of food. It is better to supply nutrient to them only as they actually need it; this is the way to get maximum growth per pound of fertilizer because the nutrient is used in the most efficient way.

All this points to the need for a nitrogen fertilizer that dissolves slowly. Unfortunately, all the nitrogen compounds that are cheap and easy to make dissolve fast. Chemists have found that the best way to get a slow dissolving rate is to use big, complex molecules of the organic type, but big, complex molecules are expensive to make.

A very large amount of research has been done on reducing fertilizer dissolution rate but the goal of slow release plus low price has not yet been achieved. The most successful commercial materials have been reaction products of urea with an aldehyde, a combination that forms compounds of reduced solubility. In the United States, for example, a product with the tradename "ureaform" is made by reacting urea with formaldehyde (HCHO); a mixture of methylene-urea polymers of varying molecular weights, and therefore of varying dissolution rate, is formed. But the formaldehyde adds raw material cost, the manufacturing process is expensive, and the nitrogen content—as compared to the original urea—is reduced. All this makes the ureaform sell for a higher price than most farmers can afford. Most of it goes to lawns and golf courses as a "specialty" turf fertilizer, where price is not a major consideration because appearance rather than crop yield is the main criterion.

Research goes on to find a cheaper slow-release fertilizer. One of the most promising departures in recent years is putting a thin, impervious coating on a standard material, such as urea or ammonium nitrate, to keep water out of the granule after it is placed in the soil. In other words, we "paint" the outside of the granule to keep moisture out.

This may sound easy but it is far from it. For one thing, if you look at a fertilizer granule through a microscope, you see a very rugged landscape, full of deep valleys and with masses of crystals projecting up like miniature mountains. When the coating is applied it tends to fill the valleys first, and if a peak is left projecting above the protective surface we might as well have not applied any coating at all, for soil moisture will quickly attack the peak, dissolve it, and move on into the granule through the opening.

Another thing working against us is the geometry of the granules, which can be regarded as spheres for purposes of discussion. A layer on the surface of a sphere makes up a considerably larger proportion of the volume than it does of the diameter, which is easy to see when we consider that the volume varies with the cube of the diameter. If we increase the diameter by only one-tenth by putting on a layer, we increase the volume by about one-third. So a layer thick enough to fill the granule valleys and cover the peaks deep enough takes a large amount of coating material.

Many types of coating materials, including plastics, petroleum byproducts, waxes, and various others, have been tried. One of the more promising is sulfur, which, although you might normally think of it as a powdery, yellow solid, will melt and form a smooth, fairly impervious film when sprayed on a fertilizer pellet. The chemists who developed sulfur coating (in 1965–68) had a hard time. After they learned how to "spray paint" the granules, which was not easy because both granules and sulfur have to be at the right temperature to get the sulfur to spread over the granule without running off or causing sticking, they found that tiny cracks or holes that developed in the coating after cooling allowed moisture to come in too fast. They solved this by filling the cracks with a wax in a second spraying. Then when the granules were placed in the soil another problem developed; the rate of dissolution was much faster than laboratory tests on rate of solution in water would indicate. After much cogitation, the chemists decided that this was probably due to soil bacteria that were dining on the wax sealant. The bacteria were disposed of by putting a microbicide such as coal tar oil in the wax, and this finally completed the development. The sulfur-wax-tar oil coating was quite successful, releasing the urea slowly and uniformly over a period of several months.

Pilot plant development of the sulfur-coating method is

continuing; commercial production before long is likely.

Still another, and completely different, idea for getting slow release has been developed recently. Since, as we learned earlier, most plants wait until ammonia-type nitrogen is oxidized to nitrate before they take it up, if the oxidation could be delayed we would have the equivalent of slow release even though the granules dissolved rapidly on contact with the soil. Such an oxidation inhibitor, an organic material of the pyridine type, has been discovered. It discourages the soil organisms that cause oxidation much as the tar oil mentioned earlier inhibits those that consume the wax sealant in the sulfur coating. The method is still in the preliminary commercial stage.

Chapter 5

Phosphate

"Bringer of light" to the ancient Greeks and "morning star" to the Romans—both were terms for phosphorus that sprang from its eerie glow in the dark. When we move into the field of plant nutrition, however, we must regretfully leave behind the phosphorescence that led to such poetic nomenclature, for phosphorus as such is not a good fertilizer; it must be combined with oxygen to form phosphate ($-PO_4$) before the plant can use it.

Fortunately, this is no problem at all because nature has already done the job for us. Phosphorus is not like nitrogen, the aloof element that floats above the earth in great quantities uncombined with any other element; phosphorus likes company, to the extent that when we have converted it to the elemental form, which is a difficult and expensive operation, we must cover it with water to keep it from rapidly reacting with oxygen in the air. If the water is removed, a violent fire soon starts and a large volume of smoke fumes off. [The "smoke" is made up of small particles of phosphorus oxide (P_2O_5).]

We do not know when phosphorus existed on the earth in elemental form, but possibly it did so in past eons when the chemistry of the earth was quite different from what it is today. If any existed it must have disappeared quickly when oxygen appeared in an uncombined form, for the two would have quickly reacted with each other, a process called oxidation. Today, all the phosphorus in the earth is tied up with other elements, mainly with oxygen in the form of phosphates.

The problem is that it is tied up too tightly. Over the course of geologic time the earth has gone through many heavings and twistings, fast and slow, that have given the phosphate ample opportunity to react with other elements in a sort of slide down the energy slope to the most unreactive and intractable compounds possible. Today most of the phosphate is in such a form, so insoluble and inert that a large amount of chemical energy must be used to pull it back to a form reactive enough for use by plants. Thus the situation is somewhat like that in converting nitrogen to a usable form; both require difficult processing to make them usable, but with the difference that for nitrogen the problem is getting it to react with something and with phosphate the difficulty is getting it unreacted.

The importance of phosphate has been emphasized in previous chapters. No life could exist without it, and large quantities are needed to grow the larger and larger crops essential for the future. With a little stretch of the imagination we can still find significance in the poetic terms of the Greeks and Romans; to a starving people phosphate can well be a "morning star" and a "bringer of light."

The world consumption of phosphate is growing rapidly, from 10,700,000 tons[1] in 1960 to 15,100,000 in 1965—a growth rate of about 8 percent per year. This is not as fast a growth as for nitrogen but a quite respectable one nevertheless. About the same rate of growth has been in effect since 1950, which indicates that consumption may continue to double every ten to fifteen years for some time to come.

Where Phosphate Comes From

There is plenty of phosphate in the earth; it is one of the more plentiful elements in the earth's crust. The trouble is that it is too well distributed. Most of it is already in the soil that grows the plants we use, but in such a low

---

[1] This is tons of P_2O_5 (phosphorus oxide), not tons of fertilizer. The various phosphate fertilizers vary widely in P_2O_5 content.

concentration, about 0.25 percent P_2O_5, that it does not support plant growth adequately without supplemental supply.

To get phosphate for use in making fertilizers, we must find it somewhere in a concentrated form. And this must be a high concentration, for a material of intermediate phosphate content, say 5 percent P_2O_5, would be too expensive to process even though it is much richer in phosphate than is the soil.

In primordial times, after earth chemistry had somewhat settled down, the phosphate must have been a part of the igneous rocks that remained after the great heat of ancient earth had subsided. Some of these rocks still remain, in the Kola Peninsula in northwestern Russia, for example, which is now one of the major sources of phosphate ore for world industry.

But in other areas the phosphate slowly dissolved over untold centuries and found its way to the sea. There it might have remained but in those eras the face of the earth was a changing thing—land masses rose and fell from convulsions within the earth and there was continual change from sea to land and back again. In such a geologic turmoil the phosphate became well distributed over most of the earth's surface.

As the earth stilled further, the phosphate had more time to build up in the oceans before they became land again and solid deposits began to form in the depths. We do not know just why this happened, but Kazakov, a Russian scientist, has theorized that calcium carbonate (limestone) pellets formed on the sea bottom and then reacted with dissolved phosphate in the water to form highly insoluble calcium phosphates. Fluorine was also present in the water and it reacted too, forming an even more complex and insoluble compound called apatite [$(3CaO \cdot P_2O_5)_3 \cdot CaF_2$]. Then finally the sea bottom heaved up again, or perhaps the water evaporated away in some slow climatic change, putting the phosphate deposit on dry land and making it accessible to man in a later age.

Another source was the tremendous mass of life in the ancient seas. The bones of the numerous species that lived in the oceans contained phosphate that, in the end, sank to the bottom and added to the beds that later became the phosphate ore deposits of modern times. Miners of such ores often find bones and teeth of early fish and animals embedded in the phosphate.

Today the oceans remain pretty well in place and in the span of recorded history little change has taken place in the earth's surface. When the fertilizer industry began, man started searching for phosphate ores. Gradually the situation became clear: nature has obligingly provided concentrated deposits of phosphate but unfortunately they are few and far between. Some countries have them but most do not.

The major known deposits of phosphate are in the United States, the U.S.S.R., and North Africa. Other deposits are scattered around the world, mainly in South America, the Middle East, South Africa, and the South Sea Islands, but they are relatively small. Asia, with its great need for food, is particularly lacking in phosphate concentrated enough to mine economically.

We must not conclude, however, that all the phosphate hidden in the earth has been found. Exploration goes on for phosphate as well as for other minerals, and a new strike of some mineral or other occurs somewhere in the world practically every day. The gold rush days are gone but men still prospect for iron, uranium, oil, phosphate, potash, and many other materials important in industry.

The United States is fortunate in phosphate. Over 30 percent of the world reserves lie in Florida, North Carolina, Tennessee, and the Rocky Mountain states of Idaho,

Utah, Montana, and Wyoming. North Africa (Tunisia, Algeria, Morocco) has even more, about 50 percent, and the U.S.S.R. deposits represent about 15 percent.

How long will our phosphate reserves last? This is a good question in regard to any mineral resource, for the concentrations of chemical compounds that nature has graciously provided will not last forever, especially since we use more of them every year. Eventually we will use up the concentrated sources—the ores, the deposits, and the oil and gas bodies—and everything will become more or less uniformly distributed back over the earth's surface and into its atmosphere; the iron will be redispersed, for example, as rust, oil as automobile fumes, coal as smoke and carbon dioxide, phosphate as insoluble compounds in the farmers soil, and great quantities of other things will flow down the rivers to the sea to wait for some modern upheaval or movement of the oceans to bring it to light again in a concentrated form.

This may be a somewhat extreme picture, but it is quite true that our modern tremendous appetite for materials is leading to depletion of our concentrated mineral sources and return to the earth in such a diluted dispersion that recovery is not economically feasible, at least as we define economic feasibility today.

We are in better shape on phosphate than some other materials. Currently we use about 50,000,000 tons of phosphate ore per year over the world. Estimates on the reserves vary widely, but about 50,000,000,000 tons seems to be as good a figure as any. This makes the arithmetic easy; clearly we have enough for a thousand years. The trouble with such a sweeping conclusion is that we don't know what the consumption will be even a few years from now or how much new phosphate will be discovered in the future.

In the industry, phosphate ore is ordinarily called

"phosphate rock," probably because the first mining was of rocklike outcroppings on the surface. Today the term "rock" is not so appropriate, for most of the deposits mined are more like sand or dirt than rock. In Florida, for example, tremendous power shovels, large enough to load a 50-car freight train in an hour, scoop out the phosphate in open-pit mining. It is usually necessary to remove from 5 to 40 feet of ordinary soil and rock, called "overburden," to expose the phosphate beds, which are normally several feet thick. As an average, about 30,000,000 tons of overburden must be removed to get at the 30,000,000 tons of phosphate material mined per year.

The 30,000,000 tons mined is not all phosphate, however; although the deposition in ancient Floridian seas concentrated the phosphate, other things settled into the beds along with it, and later movements of the surface probably promoted further contamination. Fortunately much of this can be removed merely by slurrying with water and screening and settling to remove the fine mud from the larger phosphate particles. But there is still a considerable amount of sand mixed in with the phosphate, so near in size and density to the phosphate particles that it is not separated during the mud washing operation. To separate the sand an ingenious process called "flotation" is used. First, an oil is added which, because of surface characteristics, coats out on the phosphate but not on the sand. Then the mixture is agitated with air to form a lot of bubbles. Because of the oil film, bubbles attach themselves to the phosphate particles and float them to the surface while the sand settles.

After all this washing, screening, and floating, we have removed about two tons of mud and sand for every ton of phosphate. And remember that we removed about three tons of overburden before we started work on the phosphate. But even with all this handling and processing, phosphate rock sells at only $5 to $8 per ton. Only with all the resources of mining engineering applied to refine the techniques, and with very large equipment used in the mining and concentration, could such a low cost be possible.

After locating the phosphate buried in the earth, removing the debris that has settled in the ages since the phosphate beds were first laid down, and separating out the extraneous material that settled with it or was mixed in later, what do we have? A material that to the eye still looks like dirt. Chemically, however, it is the calcium phosphate mentioned earlier, with fluorine present also (in an amount depending on the degree of exposure to fluorine when the phosphate lay on the bottom of the sea). The phosphorus content, expressed as the oxide (P_2O_5), is 30 to 35 percent.

As we might expect, phosphate from one deposit may be quite different in composition and in physical character from that mined in some other area. The history of each deposit is different, for early earth supplied a great variety of conditions for phosphate bed formation. These differences are a source of trouble today, because a process that works well with one phosphate may be difficult to operate with another. Here again nitrogen fertilizers have the advantage; atmospheric nitrogen is the same throughout the world—as uniform in Tokyo as it is in Paris.

The Sulfur Problem

Sulfur is a very important raw material in the fertilizer industry, not as a nutrient but as the starting material for an acid to use in dissolving phosphate rock. As we saw earlier, phosphate as mined is a very insoluble, intractable material, of little value as a fertilizer unless it is treated to increase solubility. This was one of the problems that the early workers such as Liebig and Kohler recognized and did something about—by treating the phosphate with sulfuric acid. Today sulfuric acid plays a major role in fertilizer technology, not only by reacting with phosphate to form superphosphate as in Liebig's day but also by reacting to form phosphoric acid, which is one of the starting materials in making triple superphosphate and ammonium phosphates.

To get sulfuric acid, we must, as a rule, first get sulfur. Sulfur is a yellow, solid material, and is unique because it is one of the few elements found in nature in an uncombined form. (In fact, nitrogen, oxygen, sulfur, carbon, and gold are about the only elements of any consequence that have escaped getting tied up with something else during the course of geologic history.) This makes sulfur easy to use, as compared, say, to iron or phosphorus, because we do not have to expend energy in untieing it before we can use it.

Most of the pure sulfur was laid down centuries ago in beds located along the Gulf Coast of the United States and Mexico. The beds are deep in the ground, much further down than the phosphate beds in Florida, so surface mining is seldom feasible and shaft mining would be very expensive. For a long time it was a puzzle how to get the sulfur out, until a method was developed that worked very well, so well, in fact, that people started calling the sulfur deposits "Frasch sulfur" because the Frasch method is the only economical way to get it out of the ground.

Frasch noted that sulfur melts at a fairly low temperature and that it is not soluble in water, so he merely drilled a hole down to the sulfur bed, put in a double pipe (a small pipe within a larger one), and pumped hot water down through the inner pipe. When the hot water got to the sulfur it melted that near the end of the pipe, and the mixture of molten, liquid sulfur and water was forced back up through the outer pipe. Then when the mixture reached the surface it was pumped out to an open area where the sulfur solidified as it cooled; the water ran off to waste or was recovered for reheating and pumping back again. By this procedure the bed of sulfur under the ground was neatly converted to a bed of sulfur on top of the ground.

This is such an inexpensive method of mining, and there was so much pure sulfur in the beds, that sulfur became an inexpensive chemical raw material. Unfortunately, this did not last. In the 1960s the fertilizer phosphate industry began to expand very rapidly and to demand more and more sulfur. As usually happens in such a situation, the price of sulfur began to climb, until it was twice what it had been a few years before. But even worse, it became apparent that the supply of pure, inexpensive Frasch sulfur could be exhausted within a generation if the voracious appetite of the fertilizer industry continued unabated.

It is always dangerous to predict that a natural resource is becoming exhausted. Someone usually comes up with a new find that extends the supply. But it does appear that we are approaching a milestone in history—the first time that the supply of a basic raw material has finally run out. This will obviously happen many times in the future, for the resources are limited but time and people are not. But if Frasch sulfur runs out it will be a new experience for modern man.

This does not mean, however, that we will not have any future source of sulfur at all. There are plenty of alternate sources, but the point is that none of them are nearly so cheap and convenient as the Frasch sulfur beds. The two main alternate sources are pyrites, an iron sulfide (FeS_2) ore found in many places around the world, and sour gas, which is natural gas containing hydrogen sulfide (H_2S) along with the usual methane (CH_4). Both require expensive processing to get sulfur or sulfuric acid from them.

The conversion processes are well worked out, however, and both are widely used as sulfur sources.

But even these are exhaustible. In fact, one estimate (Fig. 7) predicts that we will run out of all three—Frasch sulfur, pyrites, and sour gas—by 1990.

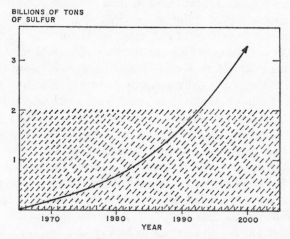

Fig. 7 The disturbing story of our sulfur supply. The lower part of the chart, below the 2,000,000,000 ton line, is the sulfur we have in forms that we know how to use economically. The projected consumption curve is exhausting this supply fast; by about 1990 it will all be gone. By then we must learn how to recover sulfur from materials such as gypsum that we do not now use.

What can we do then? Get sulfur from the sea? Hardly, for the concentration is so low, just as it is in most places on dry land, that processing costs would be prohibitive. We would most likely turn to the large deposits of gypsum (calcium sulfate; $CaSO_4$) found in many places. Gypsum is already being mined but mainly to make the wallboard used for the walls of most homes. Converting it to sulfur or sulfuric acid is a difficult operation because, like phosphate, it has reacted with just about everything around and through the centuries has reached a very low energy level. But it can be done. All it takes is money, and a lot more than we have been accustomed to spending for sulfur.

All these are possibilities for the future. At present, elemental sulfur is still the main source for the fertilizer industry. So let us turn our attention back to sulfur and learn how to use it.

We will not have time to discuss sulfuric acid production in detail; that could well be the subject of another book. But since all large phosphate plants have a sulfuric acid unit as part of the installation, we will go into it briefly.

Another common term for sulfur is "brimstone," which in old English meant "burning stone." Sulfur burns readily, and this affinity for oxygen makes it easy to convert to sulfuric acid. We merely react it with oxygen and then with water.

The first step goes like this:

$$S + O_2 \longrightarrow SO_2$$

A large amount of heat is given off, just as if we were burning the carbon in coal. In fact, a sulfuric acid plant could also be called a steam boiler because the hot gases from the sulfur burner are usually cooled by passing them through the tubes of a boiler.

We still do not have enough oxygen combined with the sulfur, however, for if we added water we would get:

$$SO_2 + H_2O \longrightarrow H_2SO_3$$

This is sulfurous acid, not sulfuric acid, and is not a very good acid for our purpose. So we go through a second oxidation step, this time at high temperature and with a catalyst, for the third oxygen is not easy to put on:

$$SO_2 + 1/2\,O_2 \xrightarrow{\text{catalyst}} SO_3$$

Now we are ready for the final step:

$$SO_3 + H_2O \longrightarrow H_2SO_4$$

The resulting sulfuric acid is a very strong acid, easy to use and preferred over any other acid for acidulation of phosphate rock. We could use some other strong acid such as hydrochloric (HCl) or nitric (HNO_3), and in fact these acids are used to a limited extent, but the sulfuric has several advantages, as we shall see later.

Sulfuric acid is an important intermediate material in the manufacture of many chemical products. The great tonnages of the fertilizer industry, however, demand the largest amount—about half of all the sulfuric acid produced.

Superphosphate

When Liebig, Lawes, and Kohler first started the practice of treating natural phosphates with sulfuric acid to improve their fertilizer value, they needed a name for the new product. The history is a little dim and it is not clear who was first, but someone called it "superphosphate," presumably to indicate its superiority over ordinary untreated phosphate. Thus the first major fertilizer, and still a very important one, was christened.

This was the only name needed for a long time, but then, in 1872, the idea was conceived of using phosphoric acid rather than sulfuric acid to treat the rock. Now there were two superphosphates and two names were needed.

Various ones have been tried. The general approach in naming the older type was to use a term indicating it as the standard; hence we have the terms "ordinary superphosphate" and "normal superphosphate" to indicate the older type. Both are used but the latter is preferred. Another tack was to try to apply multiples of the nutrient content to the terminology; the new superphosphate contained about twice as much P_2O_5 as the older type, so one could be called "double superphosphate" and the other "single superphosphate." The latter term is still widely used in countries other than the United States. The term "double superphosphate" was used for some time but improvements increased the P_2O_5 content to 45–48 percent—or about three times as much as the "single superphosphate." This led to the term "triple superphosphate," which is the common term today.

When the early workers first treated phosphate with sulfuric acid, they fortuitously hit on a reaction that worked quite well even though there were no chemical engineers in that day to design and operate equipment. When one of the materials in a reacting system is a solid, the other must usually be a liquid so that the solid particles can move around and make contact with the molecules they are supposed to react with. This can be arranged by adding water to the system to dissolve one or both of the reactants. The trouble with this, however, is that if we want a solid product, as Lawes and Kohler did, we must get the water back out again, which can be an expensive and sometimes troublesome operation.

If Lawes and Kohler had been forced to boil the water out of their phosphate-acid mixture, the resulting corrosion and expense might have discouraged them completely. But the mixture obligingly dried itself. When the rock and acid were first mixed (with water added to give the necessary fluidity), a fluid slurry was formed, but after a few minutes the slurry hardened ("set up") into a solid. What was happening was that "hydrates" were being formed, that is, the new compounds took water into the molecule and as such the water was no longer "free water" and could not have a wetting or slurrying effect on the products. The chemistry goes like this:

$$[Ca_3(PO_4)_2]_3 \cdot CaF_2 + 7H_2SO_4 + 17H_2O \longrightarrow$$

phosphate   sulfuric
rock   acid

$$3CaH_4(PO_4)_2 \cdot H_2O + 7CaSO_4 \cdot 2H_2O + 2HF\uparrow$$

monocalcium   calcium   hydrogen
phosphate   sulfate   fluoride

So mixing of rock and acid, plus breaking up the hardened mass into smaller particles, were the only operations needed in making superphosphate. This was simple and could be done by the most unskilled labor.

It was soon found that one other operation should be added to improve the product quality before sale. The reaction mix hardened so fast that the larger phosphate particles did not have time to react completely before the hardening kept them from moving around and contacting the acid. The product, then, was a mixture of the desired compounds with some unreacted rock and acid that had not had time to get together. The unreacted acid made the superphosphate difficult to handle and corrosive to bags and equipment.

Because of this problem, the practice of "curing" came into use. After the hardened superphosphate was broken up, it was taken directly to a storage pile and left there about three weeks, during which time the acid slowly diffused to the phosphate rock and reacted with it.

Chemical processes were very crude in those days and manufacture of superphosphate was no exception. In a typical plant, acid was run into a brick-lined pit, finely ground phosphate was shoveled in by hand, and men standing around the pit mixed the rock and acid with rakes. After waiting until the mass had set up the men returned with shovels, dug the superphosphate out of the pit, and hauled it to the curing pile in wheelbarrows. All this was very unpleasant because, as the reaction given earlier shows, corrosive and foul-smelling fluoride gases were given off as the rock and acid reacted. This did not seem to worry anyone, for employee working conditions were not given much attention in those days. But it is reported that most of the superphosphate workers lived to a ripe old age.

The open mixing pit and hand mixing soon gave way to more mechanized and efficient equipment. A closed chamber, with a mixer mounted on top, came into use; the mixer fed the mix into the chamber through a hole in the top. For some unknown reason, the receiving chamber became known as a "den." It was certainly not the pleasant place the den in a modern home is; perhaps it got its name because, like a lion's den, it was a place to stay out of if possible.

One of the main advantages of the den was that the fluoride fumes could be vented from the top into a chimney. But after the mix had set up, the men still had to go into the den (through a removable front wall) and dig out the superphosphate. It was still unpleasant because steam and fluoride boiled out of the mass when the shovels dug into it.

The next development was a mechanical excavator, a somewhat advanced type of equipment for the day. Inventors had a field day and some very "way out" designs were patented. The type that became the most popular is still widely used today. It employs a large cutter wheel much like the paddle wheel on an old Mississippi River steamboat, except that the wheel turns on a vertical axis. The den is built like an opentop railroad car and rolls on a track; the sides and one of the end walls are removable; and the top, into which is set the mixer, is part of the fixed structure. When the den is rolled into place for filling, it fits closely under the top. After the superphosphate has set up, the sides and front end wall are removed and the den is pushed forward into the slowly revolving cutter wheel, which shaves thin slices off the face of the advancing block of superphosphate and drops them onto a conveyor belt for transfer to the curing pile. No hand work is required.

The latest designs are aimed at making the process continuous, which is usually cheaper than batch operation in modern chemical engineering practice. All of them involve a conveying step, in which the freshly mixed slurry is placed on a slowly moving endless conveyor, sets up in transit, and is disintegrated and discharged at the destination point. The usual type is a broad belt (solid or slat type) on pulleys; the mixer discharges continuously onto the belt at one end (with a dam to keep the fluid mix from running off over the near pulley), and the slurry is held in place either by the cup of the belt or by stationary sides against which the belt rubs. By the time the mix reaches the end of the belt it has set up and is shaved off, as the belt passes over the second pulley, by a miniature version of the riverboat paddle wheel.

Triple superphosphate was first produced a few years after normal superphosphate and is made in much the same way; about the only difference is that the mix sets up faster and therefore a shorter conveyor can be used. The main reaction that takes place in manufacture of triple superphosphate is:

$$[Ca_3(PO_4)_2]_3CaF_2 + 14H_3PO_4 + 10H_2O \longrightarrow$$
$$10CaH_4(PO_4)_2 \cdot H_2O + 2HF \uparrow$$

It can be seen that this is exactly what takes place in normal superphosphate manufacture, except that no calcium sulfate is formed. Hence triple superphosphate, in effect, is normal superphosphate with the calcium sulfate left out, which raises the P_2O_5 content by over twofold.

Normal superphosphate has had a very successful history. Soon after it was invented in 1831 it became the leading phosphate fertilizer and it has held that position to the present day. While other early fertilizers rose and fell, the low cost and simple manufacturing method have kept normal superphosphate at the top. But it is now steadily losing ground as the modern trend to high nutrient content brings in more and more of the highly concentrated materials such as triple superphosphate and ammonium phosphate. The heyday of normal superphosphate was in the early decades of the present century, when it supplied over 90 percent of the fertilizer phosphate in the United States. After a long and gradual decline, in 1964 it lost first place. It is still the leader on a world basis, but by 1965 had dropped to only 45 percent of world phosphate, less than half the total. At the present rate of decline, one of its modern competitors, probably ammonium phosphate, will take over the world lead in fifteen to twenty years.

Triple superphosphate has done considerably better. Starting from practically nothing in the early 1930s, it rose to 14 percent of the total world supply by 1962. Since then it has barely held its own, however, as ammonium phosphate and other modern phosphates increased in popularity. Production of triple superphosphate has increased each year, but the others have grown faster and have taken up the slack left by the declining normal superphosphate, so that triple has not been able to gain on a percentage basis.

The superphosphates remain as good, basic fertilizers, once preeminent and still in the lead—but now retreating before the newcomers. They will remain very important phosphates, however, for a long time to come.

Phosphoric Acid

To make the modern highly concentrated fertilizers such as triple, super, and ammonium phosphate, we must have phosphoric acid, a material that is growing rapidly in importance in the fertilizer industry.

Phosphoric acid is not a new material; in fact, it is older than normal superphosphate because it was one of the early discoveries in the history of chemistry, long before fertilizers were given much attention. Boyle made it from phosphorus in 1698 and there was limited commercial production in the eighteenth and early nineteenth centuries. One of the earliest ventures into the fertilizer field, possibly the first, was in Biebrich, Germany, in 1870, where a plant was built to make phosphoric acid and react it with phosphate rock to make triple superphosphate.

After this, phosphoric acid soon became a basic chemical, widely used both in fertilizer and chemical production. Today the soap, detergent, and animal feed industries, as well as the fertilizer industry, depend heavily on phosphoric acid as a basic raw material.

Since the earliest days, two radically different routes have been followed in making phosphoric acid. We will discuss these separately because they have so little in common with each other.

The acid route is the most common method and the one of paramount importance in the fertilizer industry. Practically all the phosphoric acid that goes into triple superphosphate and ammonium phosphates is made in this way.

The early chemists who worked with phosphorus and phosphates found that when bones were treated with enough sulfuric acid a new acid was formed, along with a solid that was quite different from the initial bone particles. Later, when the fertilizer pioneers treated bones and phosphate rock with sulfuric acid to make superphosphate, they noted the same thing; when more than the usual amount of sulfuric acid was used, the mixture did not set up like superphosphate but remained a suspension of the new solid in the new acid.

What was happening was formation of phosphoric acid and calcium sulfate.

$$[Ca_3(PO_4)_2]_3CaF_2 + 10H_2SO_4 + 20H_2O \longrightarrow$$

phosphate rock   sulfuric
                 acid

$$6H_3PO_4 + 10CaSO_4 \cdot 2H_2O + 2HF \uparrow$$

phos-   calcium
phoric   sulfate
acid

Thus one acid disappears and another is formed, which is what we want to happen in this case. The reason it works chemically is that sulfuric acid is a stronger acid than phosphoric. It needs calcium, ammonium, sodium, or almost any other positive ion to satisfy its chemical potential, so it is able to take the calcium in the phosphate rock away from the phosphate—forming calcium sulfate rather than calcium phosphate. The phosphate is forced to take the hydrogen ions that the sulfuric acid leaves behind and thus becomes phosphoric acid.

It should be noted that we cannot make sulfuric acid in this way, by reacting calcium sulfate with some other acid.

$$CaSO_4 + H_2X \longrightarrow H_2SO_4 + CaX$$

The reason is that there is no acid available stronger than sulfuric, that could take the calcium away from the sulfate and make the sulfate take over the hydrogen ions to form sulfuric acid.

The early workers found that although the product slurry of calcium sulfate in phosphoric acid was easy to make, it was far from easy to get the two products separated. The calcium sulfate particles were so fine that the mixture acted something like a thin mud, from which separation of a clear liquid was very difficult.

Then came a long and tedious period of process and equipment development, somewhat like the development periods for ammonia and urea that we have talked about earlier—except that phosphoric acid took longer. The early developers were up against the problem of crystallization, something quite different from the problems in ammonia and urea production; crystallization is so touchy an operation that despairing chemical engineers have referred to it as more of an art than a science.

One of the main objectives in making phosphoric acid is to make it concentrated, for any water put in must be eventually taken out again if a solid fertilizer is to be the product. As far as the reaction is concerned, there is no need for water other than the 20 molecules put in to hydrate the calcium sulfate (see main reaction above). Very little water comes in with the sulfuric acid for it is made in very concentrated form, on the order of 98 percent (2 percent water). So it should be possible, theoretically at least, to make phosphoric acid just as concentrated as sulfuric.

Unfortunately, phosphoric acid is not fluid like sulfuric unless it is dissolved in water; the usual commercial composition is about 75 percent acid and 25 percent water. But even more important, water is needed in the making of the acid to keep the system fluid enough for growing large crystals. Unless a large quantity of water is present, the crystals produced are too fine for good separation.

The problem comes from the process called nucleation. When phosphate rock is treated with sulfuric acid, it first dissolves in the liquid acid and calcium sulfate is formed in the solution. The calcium sulfate has such limited solubility, however, that there is a powerful driving force for molecules to get together in clumps called nuclei and get themselves out of solution. When in solution the molecules swim about more or less separately but only a certain number can do this; when there are too many present—in other words, when the solubility is exceeded—the nuclei begin to form and to grow. They do not immediately become crystals, however, for in the early stages of growth they are too small to be visible. But if all goes well, they keep joining up with other molecules until they have grown to a size large enough to be called a crystal.

What controls the size to which the crystals grow? Many things, too many for a full discussion here; crystallization is a very complex mechanism, not yet fully understood. But one of the major factors is the amount of water in the system. When there is little water present in phosphoric acid production, for example, the rapidly forming calcium sulfate molecules are so jammed together—that is, the solubility is exceeded so far—that millions of nuclei form almost instantaneously to relieve the pressure. Then when they start to grow the growth is limited because there are too many nuclei for the remaining molecules that can be coaxed out of solution. But with adequate water in the system there is much less crowding in the beginning and not so many nuclei form. Then, as they grow, the unattached molecules find it easier to join up with an existing nucleus than to get together with neighbors and form a new one.

Even so, it is hard to grow calcium sulfate to a very large crystal size. Ammonium sulfate, for example, can be grown to pinhead size without much trouble but calcium sulfate, even under the best conditions, seldom exceeds a particle size roughly comparable to very fine sand.

The early workers had to use very dilute sulfuric acid (about 16 percent acid and 84 percent water) and even then they had trouble in separating the calcium sulfate from the product phosphoric acid. Large crystals can be separated merely by settling but theirs were too small for this. They resorted to filtration, which is simply straining through a cloth. Again, however, the crystals were so fine that they built up on the cloth and slowed down the flow of liquid, so much so that the filtration rate dropped off to an intolerably low level. The next step was pressure filtration in a device called a filter press; the cloth was placed on a heavy perforated support so that pressure could be applied to the slurry to push the acid through the bed of crystals at a faster rate. This worked fairly well and was the standard method for many years.

There were two things wrong, however, that made the early method quite expensive. For one thing, it was a batch process; that is, a quantity of slurry was placed in the filter, the pressure turned on until the acid had been forced through, and then the filter opened again to receive a new batch. This was a time-consuming operation, as most batch processes are. In modern engineering, processes usually run continuously, like the ammonia and urea processes discussed earlier, and therefore make more product per dollar invested in equipment and spent for labor.

The other drawback was the very low concentration of the phosphoric acid produced, on the order of 10 to 15 percent; part of this was due to the batch washing required to remove acid adhering to the solid particles. Since 75 percent acid was needed in making triple superphosphate (so the triple would set up and cure without a special drying operation), a large amount of water had to be removed from the dilute acid. This was accomplished, in a very cumbersome way, by heating in open lead-lined pans.

Not much further progress was made in production of wet process acid, as the product came to be called, until 1915, when the Dorr Company developed a continuous method; phosphate rock was treated in a series of tanks and the calcium sulfate was separated first in a series of settling tanks and later in a continuous filter, both with counter-current washing. Pressure was still used in the filtration but in the form of a vacuum applied on the outlet side of the filter cloth, which worked much better.

The Dorr process was fully continuous and therefore reduced production cost. Moreover, the new reaction system and the countercurrent washing brought the acid concentration up from the time-honored 10–15 percent to 30–34 percent.

In the years since the first continuous plant was built, research and development people have worked steadily on refining the tricky crystallization process with the aim of increasing acid concentration without reducing crystal size. They have been eminently successful; today 44 percent acid can be made at filtering rates even faster than those of the past. Much of the progress has been made by gaining a better understanding of the complex chemistry involved in the dissolution of phosphate rock in sulfuric acid and in the calcium sulfate-phosphoric acid-water system ($CaSO_4$-H_3PO_4-H_2O). Only by a careful tuning of all the variables can production of an acid as concentrated as 44 percent be achieved.

Filter design has also been improved greatly. Today the filters are far different both in design and operation from the filter presses of a hundred years ago. The major type, particularly in the larger plants, is a sort of merry-go-round shaped much like a pie, with filter pans corresponding to the pieces of the pie. Each pan is a filter in itself, with filter cloth in the bottom and vacuum applied underneath. Reacted slurry flows from a spout continuously into the filter as it turns, filling each pan as it passes by. The vacuum sucks the product acid out rapidly, and the pan then, without stopping, goes through a series of countercurrent washings. The fresh wash water is applied after the pan has almost completed the circuit, and after most of the adhering acid has been washed out. The water goes through the solids cake, is collected by a complicated valve system underneath, and is then pumped back up and onto the next pan behind. This procedure is repeated, the water picking up some acid each time, so that each pan gets three washings, first with medium-strength acid, then with weak acid, and finally with fresh water.

But what to do with the wash water after it has gone through the three washings and become medium-strength acid? We cannot add it to the product acid because this would give dilution and dilution is what we are trying to avoid. The answer is simple; we send it back to the front end of the system, where we have to add some water anyway in dissolving the rock in sulfuric acid.

After the pan we were following goes through the fresh water wash it has finished its job and is ready for another trip. But we must get rid of the calcium sulfate—which is easily done by turning the pan over and letting the filter cake drop out. (The pan is mounted on a rotating mechanism that allows it to turn on a radial axis.) Then the pan is turned back into position and moves under the spout to get another load of slurry.

This particular filter is popular because, unlike many other designs, it can be built in very large sizes. Like ammonia plants, phosphoric acid plants have grown up into giants in the 1960s. It is not unusual for single production units to make as much as 1300 tons of acid per day (H_3PO_4 basis; water is not counted). This is part of the general trend to large plant size as a way of reducing capital and operating costs per ton of acid produced.

But we are still not through when the filtration is finished. Something must be done with the calcium sulfate, which is usually called gypsum in the industry. This is quite a problem for there is so much of it. For the 1300 tons of acid mentioned above, we must get rid of about 5000 tons of gypsum. It is not good for anything much, although research people have worked for years trying to find a use for it. So we must pile it up somewhere or, if our plant happens to be near the ocean, we can perhaps solve the problem by pumping or hauling it out to sea. Usually we must find some space for a disposal pile. These are becoming a problem because they grow higher and higher, some now approaching a hundred feet. If someone in the future finds a good use for byproduct gypsum, he will at least have it all neatly collected and waiting for him.

Our next problem is to concentrate the acid, for although it is much more concentrated than in the past it is still not as strong as we need it. The concentration step has also been highly refined over the past century. Instead of the open pans used by the early producers, we now have recirculating, vacuum-type evaporators. The acid is pumped through tubes where it is heated with steam on the other side of the tubes, and then is passed into a chamber where the vacuum flashes off part of the water. Part of the acid is withdrawn as product and the rest is recycled, with fresh acid from the filter added before pumping through the heating tubes again. Production rate is high and the corrosion and encrustation problems of the past have been greatly reduced.

Today the acid route to phosphoric acid is well-developed and efficient but research still goes on. Processes to make up to 58 percent acid have been developed and tested on a small scale but are not yet in commercial use. Research is proceeding also on making a purer acid, since one of the main drawbacks of wet-process acid is the load of impurities (mainly fluorides and iron and aluminum compounds) picked up from the phosphate rock.

The furnace route, as we have said, is entirely different. Here we use elemental phosphorus as the starting material, much as we use sulfur in making sulfuric acid. Unlike sulfuric acid, however, convenient deposits of phosphorus are not naturally available, and if they were, the phosphorus would probably have reacted with something by now anyway.

So we must take phosphate rock, a thoroughly reacted, low-energy compound of phosphorus, and bring it back to the elemental form. As might be expected, this takes a tremendous lot of energy. We must do it in a furnace, at such a high temperature that the reaction takes place in a molten mass at white heat. And, as in the acid route, we must have an acidic material that will tie up the calcium and remove it from the system. In the furnace process, we can use silica—ordinary sandstone rock—which, of course, is a very cheap raw material. But we have to have something further, a material we call a reducing agent, for the phosphorus is tied up with oxygen and we have to get the oxygen off, which we did not have to do in the acid route.

The reaction goes like this:

$$[Ca_3(PO_4)_2]_3CaF_2 + 10.5SiO_2 + 15C \longrightarrow 1.5P_4 \uparrow$$

Phosphate　　　　　Silica　　Carbon　　　Phos-
rock　　　　　　　　　　　　　　　　　　phorus

$$+ 10CaSiO_3 + 15CO \uparrow + 0.5SiF_4 \uparrow$$

Calcium　　　Carbon
silicate　　monoxide

Here the carbon, supplied to the furnace as coke, acts as the reducing agent and ties up the oxygen.

As the equation shows, everything but the calcium silicate (called slag) comes out of the furnace as a gas. How then can we separate the phosphorus from the carbon monoxide? By cooling, since the phosphorus is a solid at ordinary temperature but carbon monoxide is a gas. This separates the phosphorus in a satisfactory way but the carbon monoxide leaving the cooler-condenser cannot be released to the atmosphere because it is highly poisonous. It burns easily, so the usual practice is to burn it in some associated operation requiring heat, thus converting it to harmless carbon dioxide.

The condensed phosphorus is not an easy material to handle. It burns spontaneously on exposure to air and causes serious burns if it gets on the skin. The general practice is to store it in tanks under a layer of water (the phosphorus is insoluble) and to handle it only with pumps.

This leaves the calcium silicate slag. Like calcium sulfate from the acid route, it is not worth much for anything and therefore is usually sluiced out to a disposal pile. And, also like calcium sulfate, there are tremendous quantities of it that grow into young mountains around phosphorus plants. Some uses have been developed, such as construction aggregate and liming agent for soil, but these have not made much of a dent in the total.

We have not said anything yet about the type of furnace. Although other types have been used in the past, all modern phosphorus production is in electric furnaces. The furnace is a large chamber lined with carbon blocks in the lower part and with carbon electrodes extending down through the roof. The charge—rock, silica, and coke—is also fed (continuously) through the roof. Electric current passing from the electrodes to the carbon blocks heats the charge and forms a molten pool in the bottom. The phosphorus formed boils off and leaves with the furnace gases, and the molten slag is tapped out from time to time.

Development of the furnace process has been a long and painful struggle, in common with the other basic chemical processes. A glassmaker, Hennig Brand, discovered phosphorus in 1669, not, however, in connection with his glassmaking work but in a side excursion into alchemy. He was looking for the "philosopher's stone" that would turn ordinary metal into gold. This seems laughable today but Brand made a major contribution when he accidentally produced a material that glowed in the dark, later called phosphorus and found to be an element of great importance.

Brand thought he had something, because of the mysterious "cold light," and tried to keep his production method secret. But alchemists were pretty good spies apparently, for soon others had learned how to make the new material. However, for a long time phosphorus remained mainly a laboratory curiosity; it did not help much in developing the philosopher's stone and Brand's production method, heating a mixture of coal and urine, was hardly suited to large-scale manufacture for commercial use.

The modern technology might be said to have begun in 1877, when James Burgess Readman in England started up a small experimental furnace to make phosphorus by heating a mixture of phosphate rock, sand, and coke. Then in 1890, Albright and Wilson, using Readman's patents, built in England the first industrial electric furnace and started phosphorus production that has continued to the present.

Since then many improvements have been made. The problem of removing dust from the gas before condensing the phosphorus has been solved by using an electrostatic precipitator, wires charged with electricity that pull fine dust particles out of the gas. Improved methods of preparing the furnace charge have been developed; the materials must be in lump form to avoid being blown out of the furnace. And the size of individual furnaces has increased by a very large degree, now up to 70,000 kilowatts.

So far we have only phosphorus, which we must convert to phosphoric acid. This is the easy part of the operation for, as with sulfur, we can make the acid merely by burning the phosphorus and catching the resulting oxide in water. In fact, the job is easier than with sulfur, for phosphorus oxidizes completely and quickly in a simple burner but sulfur requires a catalyst to get the last oxygen atom attached.

Phosphorus burners and hydrators have also gone through a period of development. Corrosion has been the major problem because of the high temperature used and the corrosive character of the acid. Modern units, however, which are generally made of stainless steel, give good service because of the attention given in the design to adequate cooling of surfaces exposed to both acid and high temperature.

Why are there two methods of making phosphoric acid? One must be cheaper than the other so why not use it exclusively? This is a good question, and up until a decade or so ago we would have left the furnace acid discussion out of this book because it is more expensive and because up until that time very little fertilizer phosphate had been made by the furnace method.

The main reason for the furnace route is that it makes pure acid, and pure acid is necessary if we have in mind making detergents or other phosphate products in the commercial chemical field. Fertilizers do not have to be pure, however, so there has been little incentive to use anything other than the impure but cheaper wet-process acid. One of the factors that has changed this has been the rise of liquid mixed fertilizers which, beginning in the mid-1950s, have grown to an important place in the fertilizer supply pattern. We shall have more to say about liquid mixes later; it is enough to note here that this type of fertilizer does need to be fairly pure, or at least free of solid impurities, for trouble-free handling. Hence furnace acid has moved into the fertilizer field mainly through the liquid-mix door.

There are other factors that are improving the position of furnace acid as a fertilizer raw material. One is the growing popularity of superphosphoric acid (see discussion a little later), which does not cost any more to make than ordinary acid if the furnace route is used; wet-process superphosphoric acid, on the other hand, costs considerably more than ordinary wet acid because of the expensive heating step.

But even more important, the runaway cost of sulfur is rapidly closing the cost gap between the two acids, and has already closed it in some places. Furnace plants are under construction that will produce acid mainly for the fertilizer industry. The increasing cost of sulfur, possible lower cost of electric power by the nuclear route, and ability of the furnace process to use low-grade phosphate rock are all pushing the furnace method toward a fully competitive position.

Polyphosphoric acid is the latest development in the phosphoric acid field. The difference between this acid and ordinary acid is a chemical one. Ordinary acid, which in chemical terms is orthophosphoric acid, is put together like this:

$$
\begin{array}{c}
O \\
\| \\
H-O-P-O-H \\
| \\
O-H
\end{array}
$$

But if the orthophosphoric acid is heated high enough it will split out water and form a double acid molecule.

$$H-O-\underset{\underset{O-H}{|}}{\overset{\overset{O}{\|}}{P}}-O-H + H-O-\underset{\underset{O-H}{|}}{\overset{\overset{O}{\|}}{P}}-O-H \xrightarrow{\text{Heat}}$$

$$H-O-\underset{\underset{O-H}{|}}{\overset{\overset{O}{\|}}{P}}-O-\underset{\underset{O-H}{|}}{\overset{\overset{O}{\|}}{P}}-O-H + H_2O$$

The new acid is called pyrophosphoric acid. Other types also form on heating:

$$3H_3PO_4 \xrightarrow{\text{Heat}} H_5P_3O_{10} + 2H_2O$$

$$4H_3PO_4 \xrightarrow{\text{Heat}} H_6P_4O_{13} + 3H_2O$$

And so on. The acids can keep splitting off water and joining together until very long chains, containing hundreds of phosphorus atoms, are formed. The general name for these is "polyphosphoric acid" although each has its own name such as pyro, tripoly, tetropoly, and so on.

In practice, the commercial product is always a mixture of these various polyphosphoric acids, with the shorter chains predominating. The common name, as we might expect, is "superphosphoric acid," indicating that it is better than ordinary acid—just as Lawes named his product superphosphate to distinguish it from the ordinary phosphate of the day.

Why is the superphosphoric acid better than the ordinary type? For one thing, it is more concentrated. As we have seen, acid containing 100 percent H_3PO_4 (ordinary acid) is not usable because it would be a solid or a non-flowable liquid; super acid, on the other hand, is a liquid at ordinary temperature and therefore can be used without diluting with water. (Adding water would be hopeless anyway, for it would change the superphosphoric acid back to ordinary acid.) The concentration of the super-phosphoric acid must be expressed in terms of P_2O_5 content, for H_3PO_4 content no longer has any significance. Ordinary orthophosphoric acid, which normally contains 75 percent H_3PO_4, contains about 54 percent P_2O_5; in contrast, the P_2O_5 content of superphosphoric acid is 76 percent.

The higher concentration makes superphosphoric acid cheaper to ship. There are also other advantages, that we shall discuss later, when fertilizers are made from the acid.

Superphosphoric acid is made in two ways, as we might expect, depending on whether we are following the acid or furnace route. It is all a matter of water content. If we have made ordinary acid by the acid route, we heat it to boil out all of the free water rather than part of it, and then heat further to split water out of the molecules. If we are operating a furnace plant, the job is much easier; after the phosphorus is burned to the oxide, we merely cut back on the amount of water used in converting the oxide to acid, adding only enough to supply the hydrogen and oxygen atoms required in the polyphosphoric acids formed.

Superphosphoric acid came on the fertilizer scene in the mid-1950s. It is already a commercial fertilizer material of some significance and its use is expected to grow, in keeping with the trend to higher nutrient concentration and to labor-saving techniques in the fertilizer field.

CHAPTER 6

Potash

We have been a little critical of nature so far in regard to the raw materials that man has inherited from the past, blaming her for the inert nature of nitrogen and phosphate rock and for the shortage of sulfur. But there is little to complain about when we come to potash, for it is one of the most plentiful of the raw materials that nature has concentrated in pockets over the surface of the earth. The potash deposits are very large pockets indeed, and, except for treatment to remove associated salts, are ready to use as a fertilizer without any chemical processing at all.

Like phosphate, in the early history of the earth potash dissolved from the rocks and flowed with the creeks and rivers to the sea. But unlike phosphate, it did not join up with limestone and fluorine to form insoluble material that settled to the bottom and, after the sea moved away, became the phosphate beds that make up our phosphate reserves today. Potash picked a more reactive partner, chlorine—or at least a good part of it did, for many other compounds were formed also. The resulting potassium chloride was quite soluble and over the centuries it accumulated in the sea water. When the sea moved on somewhere else because of shiftings in the earth's crust, the potash went with it but the phosphate was left behind.

But sometimes it happened that an arm of the sea was cut off and became a land-locked lake or inland sea. Or, as the earth buckled and twisted, a fresh-water lake might form and gradually become loaded with potash and other salts. (Modern examples are the Great Salt Lake and the Dead Sea.) Then came changes in the climate that reduced the rainfall; the rivers that fed these bodies of water dwindled away and the inland sea itself disappeared as the sun evaporated water from its surface and the winds carried the vapor away to other parts of the world.

Thus were formed the great salt beds that we mine today. They are not all one material, of course, for many materials dissolved from the ancient rocks and were carried into the oceans—compounds of sodium, calcium, and magnesium as well as potassium; and sulfates, carbonates, and borates as well as chlorides. All of them crystallized when the water evaporated, but fortunately there were differences in solubility, so they came out at different times and therefore formed separate layers as the evaporation proceeded. This gave some degree of separation although it was by no means perfect. Unfortunately, potassium chloride and sodium chloride (common salt) were close enough in solubility that they came out together, particularly after most of the sodium chloride had crystallized out. An example of this is a bed in Saskatchewan (Canada) that is some 600 feet thick. The lower two-thirds is mainly sodium chloride and the upper third is a mixture of potassium and sodium chlorides.

Most of the beds mined for potash are mixtures of this type. The material as mined usually contains about 20 to 25 percent potassium chloride and 70 to 75 percent sodium chloride.

Potash has been known and used for over 3000 years but the early peoples, of course, knew nothing about the old lake beds buried beneath the deep layers of useless material accumulated through the centuries. The common source of potash was the ashes of plants, which contain potash because the plants mine it from the soil. Aristotle (about 350 B.C.) described the practice in Italy of burning bulrushes, dissolving the ashes in water, and evaporating the water to give a mixture containing potash. In fact, this type of operation was the source of the name "potash"—"pot" (for evaporating the ash solution) plus "ash." Making potash in this way was still a common practice in the pioneer days of America. Housewives leached ashes with water and mixed the resulting potash solution with fat to make a crude form of soap.

Mining of potash did not develop to any significant degree until about the middle of the nineteenth century, when in 1843 workmen drilling for common salt in Germany tapped into a bed that contained potash as well as salt. This turned out to be much more profitable than the pure salt they were after because the potash developed into a higher priced material. The time of the discovery was just right, because Liebig had just expounded his new theories on the nutrition of plants and the world was ready to begin fertilizing the soil in earnest. In less than two decades, potash manufacture became an important industry in Germany.

In the years that followed, the general exploration for minerals over the world uncovered many new beds of potash. The German deposits were explored further and found to be very extensive, covering most of Germany and extending westward into France. Today these deposits are one of the major world sources.

In the United States it was known that brines such as those in Searles Lake in California were heavily laden with potash but there were no identified beds of solid potash such as in Germany. Then in 1912 well diggers in Texas found a potash brine rather than the pure water they were after, which no doubt was a disappointment to them but was a good thing for the country in general. This early find stimulated exploration and in 1921 potash was found near Carlsbad, New Mexico. Today this deposit is the major one being mined in the United States and is one of the most important in the world. In prehistoric times there was a great inland sea in this region, now known as the Permian Basin. During the last epoch of its life, the prevailing winds shifted and the sea began to die as evaporation gradually won out over rainfall. Finally the last of the water disappeared, and it was in this last stage that the potash crystallized—into beds sometimes 200 feet or more thick. The miners who work in these beds today can follow the last days of the vanishing sea by the signs in the strata of the winds and storms and calms.

The brine from Searles Lake is another important source of potash. To the tourist, waters such as those in the salty lakes, particularly the Great Salt Lake, are of interest mainly because they are so dense that one can float in them easily. But they are also a very important natural resource for they contain soluble minerals leached from surrounding areas over hundreds of centuries. The brines are truly a treasure house of nature, concentrated and conveniently located for use by man.

The winning of values from Searles Lake by the early developers is one of the more interesting stories in the history of applied chemistry. Remember that in the solid deposits left by the ancient dried-up lakes and seas, the various compounds in the water crystallized out more or less separately because of differences in solubility and a rough separation thereby was obtained. But in the Searles Lake water they are all still there together and the job is to separate them. Nature's method cannot be used very well for it takes too many centuries.

The chemists who developed the method now used at Searles Lake had a very complex problem in chemistry on their hands. There were several compounds in the brine, of varying solubility, and the concentration of each had an effect on the solubility of the others. There was little help from the work of earlier chemists for no one had ever studied such a complex system before. So the Searles Lake chemists studied it, and worked out a combination of process steps—evaporation, crystallization, heating, cooling, carbonation, and filtration—by which they produced not only fertilizer and chemical grades of potash but also sodium carbonate, sodium sulfate, lithium compounds, and borax. The process was eminently successful; it is a tribute to the early workers that they could tune such a complicated and delicately balanced method finely enough to make all these separations cleanly and at low cost.

The Great Salt Lake is another well-laden storehouse but unfortunately the concentration of potash is not nearly so high as in Searles Lake. Nevertheless, there are 100,-000,000 to 150,000,000 tons of potash in the Great Salt Lake, which makes it an interesting possibility for the future.

Before someone suggests the oceans as an obvious place to get potash, remember that the situation is different from that of land-locked seas in the arid areas of the world. Although the oceans are salty from minerals leached from the land, they are not being concentrated by losing ground to evaporation; moisture evaporated from the surface is brought back again by the rivers and the large influx of fresh water keeps the salt concentration down. It would take over 60 tons of sea water to give as much potash as can be obtained from one ton of Searles Lake brine.

The latest potash development is in Canada. Discovery of potash there is an example of the part oil companies play in uncovering the mineral resources of the world. Oil is so valuable and so sought after that drillers sink shafts in great numbers, anywhere that even a minor indication raises hopes of a strike. Sometimes they find it and sometimes they don't; but in drilling even dead holes they often find other things as the drill bits chew down through the layers of earth and stone and minerals laid down in past epochs. The drill brings up a core that geologists study carefully, for it is a "history" of prehistoric earth, a record of the geologic changes that concentrated valuable minerals in pockets and layers.

In 1943 oil drillers in Saskatchewan found potash in a core. In the next few years other similar finds were made, and it soon became evident that a half mile or more under the Saskatchewan and Alberta prairies lies one of the largest potash deposits in the world. Moreover, it is generally of higher grade than that found in the United States and in Europe. Although exploration is by no means complete, it appears that in Saskatchewan alone there is over 50,-000,000,000 tons—enough for about 2500 years at the present rate of world consumption.

Another area with great potash reserves is the U.S.S.R., where there are many brine lakes and large deposits—as well as large unexplored areas that could well contain potash beds.

We have talked so far about where the potash is, but having found it how do we get it out? It is usually from 500 to 3500 feet below the surface, so the phosphate industry practice of stripping off the overburden is hardly practical. Sinking a shaft would appear to be too expensive but actually this is what is done; a hole from 8 to 18 feet in diameter is drilled down to the ore beds and shafts are then cut horizontally into the potash.

Sometimes this taxes the ingenuity of the mining engineers. In Canada, for example, shaft sinking is somewhat of a nightmare; all goes well for the first 1200 feet or so because only gravel or shale is encountered—but then comes a 200-foot layer of quicksand in which the water is under high pressure. Several potash mining projects foundered because as soon as the drills tapped into it the quicksand was pushed up by its own pressure into the shaft. The answer was to freeze the quicksand into a block of ice and then drill through the ice.

It can well be asked why potash cannot be mined by pumping water down into the ore bed as in the Frasch method for mining sulfur. It can, but the trouble is that, unlike sulfur, the potash dissolves and then we have the expense of getting the water out again. Nevertheless, one such mine is operating in Canada. Much of the potash there is over 3500 feet down, the level usually considered the maximum for shaft-type mining; at this level the increasing pressure on the shaft is a major problem and solution mining becomes the only practical method.

For solution mining or treatment of natural brines, evaporation plus crystallization is the obvious method for separating the potash from the several nonpotash compounds that are also dissolved. But what can we do to avoid the expense of evaporating water when our raw material is the solid mixture of potash and common salt that we get in shaft mining? Here again, as in the phosphate industry, we can use flotation, but with the difference that a saturated brine rather than water is used as the liquid phase so that the potash will not dissolve.

The flotation method is efficient and economical, and is widely used throughout the industry. The ore is ground, slurried with a salt brine, and passed through flotation equipment where the potash is floated to the surface and raked off. The salt is usually discarded.

This is about all there is to potash production. The hard part is finding the ancient beds in the first place, which lie far deeper than the phosphate deposits, and then getting the potash-salt mixture out. But the oil drillers with their far-ranging explorations keep finding more and more potash, and modern mining methods can meet the challenge of sending men three-quarters of a mile underground to operate ore cutting machines, or of forcing water even deeper to dissolve out the ore.

After flotation or crystallization, the potash is obtained

as almost pure potassium chloride. The flotation product (60 percent K_2O) has a small content of impurities that give it a reddish color; the crystallized product (62 percent K_2O) is pure white.

Potassium chloride is so plentiful and so cheap to mine that it supplies about 92 percent of world fertilizer potash. Most of the remainder is potassium sulfate, a mineral that was also laid down in beds eons ago. The sulfate has some advantages, in tobacco and potato growing, for example, where too much chloride is bad for quality. Unfortunately, it is found mainly in a chemical combination with magnesium sulfate, not as a simple mixture like potassium chloride and sodium chloride. Therefore flotation or recrystallization is not effective and an expensive chemical process must be used to remove the unwanted magnesium sulfate. Because of this, potassium sulfate sells at a much higher price than the chloride.

CHAPTER 7

Mixed Fertilizers

If the farmer would take the nitrogen, phosphate, and potash materials we have been talking about and mix them himself or spread them on his fields separately, our fertilizer story would be about over. But for most of his fertilizer he insists on the producer doing the mixing, not because he is lazy or stubborn but because it makes good economic sense. Mixing on the farm would require equipment to weigh the materials, a mixer, and, most important, labor to do the job. Labor is short on large, modern farms, and the cost of a thousand mixers on a thousand farms would add up to much more expense than one big mixer at a manufacturing plant.

The alternative of spreading each material separately is much more logical. The practice has made some headway but even here the practical economics can be a problem. The most economical way of handling fertilizer is in bulk rather than in bags; the farmer drives his truck to the fertilizer plant, gets a load of fertilizer already mixed, takes it back to the farm, shovels it into his fertilizer distributor, and drives the distributor across the field to apply the fertilizer. Then consider what is involved if he spreads separately. He must either partition his truck or make three trips to the fertilizer plant, and then must either make three separate trips over the field with the distributor or buy a distributor with three feed hoppers on it and set each to deliver the required amount. All this is expensive and troublesome so he much prefers to buy the fertilizer already mixed.

In 1967 farmers in the United States used almost 21,-000,000 tons of mixed fertilizer and over 14,000,000 tons of the straight, unmixed type. As we have seen earlier, most of the straight material is nitrogen fertilizer applied alongside the plant after it is up and growing, phosphate applied to pastures, or phosphate and potash spread during the fallow (nongrowing) part of the year. The fertilizer used for the main feeding of the crop just before or at planting time is almost all mixed fertilizer.

The mixed fertilizer industry is too complicated for us to explore completely in this book. Production of the straight nitrogen, phosphate, and potash materials is fairly simple and straightforward but mixed fertilizer technology is a complex assembly of chemical mixes, mechanical mixes, and combinations of the two. Let us examine first some of the chemical mixes.

Ammonia and Superphosphate: The New and the Old

Since superphosphate is the main fertilizer phosphate, it is not surprising that it supplies most of the phosphate in mixed fertilizers. Over 90 percent of the normal superphosphate produced, for example, goes into mixes.

For a long time the superphosphate was used in mixes as it came from the curing pile, without any intermediate treatment. Ammonium sulfate, mainly a byproduct of coke production, supplied most of the nitrogen in the mixes. Then about 1935 one of the major chemical companies decided there might be more of a market in the fertilizer field for ammonia and ammonium nitrate if these materials could substitute for ammonium sulfate. But how could this be done, with the ammonia a volatile liquid that had to be kept under high pressure to avoid loss as a gas? The chemists rose to the occasion and found that the ammonia would react readily with superphosphate to form a stable, nonvolatile product. Moreover, if the ammonia was dissolved in ammonium nitrate solution a pressure of only a few pounds would prevent gas loss.

Another bonus was the easy, uncomplicated reaction between the ammonia-ammonium nitrate solution (generally called ammoniating solution) and superphosphate. All that was necessary was to weigh a batch of superphosphate into a machine something like a concrete mixer, pour in the proper amount of ammoniating solution, mix for about 4 minutes, and the job was done. The product required no drying, because the solution contained little water (0.5 to 15 percent) in the first place and the heat of reaction gave an automatic drying effect.

The development of ammoniation caused a minor revolution in the fertilizer industry. Seldom has a new process combined simplicity with so many advantages. The ammoniating solution was economical and high in nitrogen content (37–49 percent vs. 21 percent for ammonium sulfate), and made the superphosphate more resistant to caking than when mixed with ammonium sulfate. Fertilizer producers took up the new practice so rapidly that ammoniating solution soon became the main supplier of nitrogen to mixed fertilizers.

Then in the early 1950s the trend to granulation brought a new problem to the ammoniation technologists. The standard ammoniation method developed earlier gave a finely divided, somewhat dusty product that began to lose favor as farmers became accustomed to the good appearance and lack of dust in granular products such as ammonium nitrate. They began to ask for mixed fertilizer in granular form also.

Fertilizers can be granulated in about the same way that a child makes mud pies—by mixing with enough water to make the particles stick together. But the child can put the pie out in the sun for several hours to let it dry, a procedure that is not practical for the fertilizer producer; he must pass the damp granules through a dryer, an expensive operation. The problem then was to get granulation during ammoniation of superphosphate without adding water that would have to be removed by drying.

The answer was to get more heat of reaction. There was plenty of ammonium nitrate in the mix, more than would ordinarily dissolve in the limited amount of water present. And the ammonium nitrate was so much more soluble at high temperature that heating the mix would make more nitrate go into solution and increase the volume of liquid phase enough to make the particles ball up into granules; it made no difference that the liquid phase was not entirely water—any liquid would do.

But how to get the temperature up? Heating by steam or by burning fuel would be expensive and require special equipment. Then how about adding some acid (phosphoric or sulfuric) to give reaction heat within the mix by reacting with part of the ammonia in the ammoniating solution. It worked, and this way of granulating mixed fertilizers became a widely used process. Potash could also be incorporated—by mixing it with the superphosphate before or during ammoniation—to make a complete fertilizer.

With the coming of granulation the old concrete-mixer type of ammoniation was no longer suitable. Equipment was needed in which the superphosphate and acid could be reacted with ammonia to give the high temperature needed without boiling out part of the ammonia. Again the development engineers came up with the answer (Fig. 8), this time a horizontal rotating drum with stationary injector tubes set longitudinally in the drum and located a few inches above the bottom. In operation the drum was about one-third full of a bed of solids—superphosphate, potassium chloride, and recycled product fines—and the liquids, acid and ammonia, were injected under the tumbling mass of solids by means of the injector tubes. Thus any ammonia escaping from the hot acid-ammonia reaction zone was absorbed by the superphosphate. When the

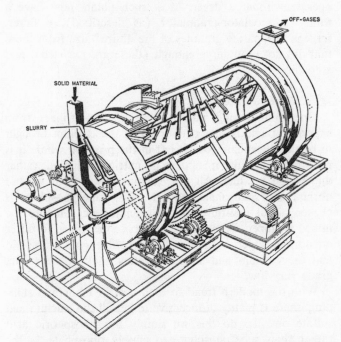

Fig. 8 Modern ammoniation of superphosphate requires special equipment. In this ammoniator drum, superphosphate plus any recycled fine solids enters at the top and ammonia is injected along the bottom of the drum. The device at the top is a scraper. A slurry inlet pipe is also shown, since in making mixed fertilizer, slurries of various types may also be used.

variables—amount of acid, amount of ammoniating solution, and rate of fines recycle—were carefully adjusted, good granulation was obtained.

By this time more and more ammoniating solution was being used to get more nitrogen into the product, so it became infeasible, at least for many of the grades made, to operate without a dryer. Most such plants now have a rotary ammoniator-granulator (as described), a dryer, screens to separate granules of the desired size from those that did not grow large enough (these are recycled), and a cooler.

Why Not Use Phosphoric Acid?

One thing wrong with making mixed fertilizer from superphosphate is that part or all of the calcium brought in by the phosphate rock is left in the product, where it is not wanted because it supplies no nutrient value but rather dilutes the product. All the calcium is left in if we use normal superphosphate, and if triple superphosphate is chosen about one-third of the calcium goes on into the mixed fertilizer. Even worse, if we base the mixed fertilizer on normal superphosphate all the sulfate goes along too and the calcium and sulfate together make the product grade very low.

With the modern trend to high cost of labor and shipping, there is plenty of incentive to get all the calcium and sulfate out. To do this we simply use phosphoric acid rather than superphosphate to supply phosphate in the mixed fertilizer; all the calcium and sulfate then is left behind in the gypsum pile at the phosphoric acid plant.

Phosphoric acid is used in the same way as superphosphate, by reacting it with ammonia and granulating the product. The result is ammonium phosphate, a very highly concentrated material that has become a major form of mixed fertilizer. The reaction can go two ways:

$$NH_3 \; + \; H_3PO_4 \longrightarrow NH_4H_2PO_4$$

ammonia   phosphoric acid   monoammonium
phosphate

$$2NH_3 \; + \; H_3PO_4 \longrightarrow (NH_4)_2HPO_4$$

diammonium
phosphate

The monoammonium phosphate is easier to make for it is difficult to force enough ammonia into the phosphoric acid to get diammonium phosphate. But the higher nutrient content of the DAP (short for diammonium phosphate in the trade) has led development people to work out the production problems.

A pure form of DAP contains 21 percent nitrogen and 54 percent P_2O_5, a total of 75 percent nutrient, but the impurities in wet-process phosphoric acid bring this down to 18-46-0, a 64 percent total. In contrast, we get a grade of about 5-18-0 when we ammoniate normal superphosphate—23 percent total nutrient; with triple superphosphate it runs about 7-44-0, or 51 percent nutrient. Thus if we make mixed fertilizer by the ammonium phosphate route, we get a concentration level considerably higher than that of the past.

Ammonium phosphate was first produced and used in 1917 but the product was ahead of its time; going from the low-grade mixed fertilizers of those days to ammonium phosphate was too much of a jump for farmers to make. Later, when the high analysis of triple superphosphate had become well accepted, it was easier to move into ammonium phosphate. Beginning in the early 1950s, consumption began to increase until by 1968 almost 2,000,000 tons of P_2O_5 was supplied by ammonium phosphate in the United States, which makes it the leading phosphate fertilizer.

Making ammonium phosphate is somewhat different from ammoniation of superphosphate, because ammoniation of phosphoric acid gives a fluid slurry of crystals and solution rather than a damp bed of solids. Ammonium phosphate production is more like making ammonium nitrate from ammonia and nitric acid, except that the reacted solution is not evaporated to a melt and granulated by prilling in a tower. The ammonium phosphate does not melt very easily and when it does the melt is sticky and hard to prill. The usual practice is to use a rotary drum granulator, which in this respect makes the operation similar to the granulation step in making granular ammoniated superphosphate.

The art of granulation—and it is more of an art than most other fertilizer processes—has been developed to an advanced degree in manufacturing of ammonium phosphate. The most popular of the various processes (Fig. 9)

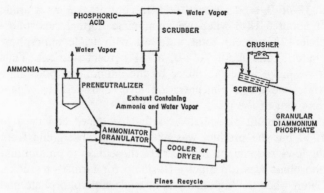

Fig. 9 Diammonium phosphate (18-46-0) is made in an operation like this. The incoming phosphoric acid first catches ammonia lost from the main reactor (the ammoniator-granulator), then is partially neutralized with ammonia in the preneutralizer, and finally is fully ammoniated in the ammoniator. Such plants make up to 50 tons per hour of diammonium phosphate.

illustrates this very well. The operation starts in a tank called the "preneutralizer" where part of the ammonia is reacted with all of the acid—in proportion to give a mixture in which the ratio of monoammonium to diammonium phosphate is about 2 to 1, which is the ratio that gives maximum solubility. Because of this, the operator can allow heat of reaction to evaporate the water down to 18–

22 percent without getting a slurry too thick to pump. The evaporated water vapor takes some ammonia along with it but this is caught in a vertical tank (called a scrubber) in which the incoming phosphoric acid, on the way to the preneutralizer, flows downward and absorbs the ammonia passing upward through the scrubber.

Now we have a slurry of partially ammoniated phosphoric acid. The next step is to run it to a rotary ammoniator-granulator much like that used in ammoniating superphosphate. In this case, however, the solids in the ammoniator are all recycled fines from the screens that separate out the product granules. The slurry is dripped from a trough-type distributor onto the bed of solids tumbling underneath as the rotary drum turns. Underneath the solids is an ammonia injector tube, like that used in superphosphate ammoniation, through which the remainder of the ammonia is injected. Here occurs the key operation of the process; the extra ammonia raises the ammonia to acid ratio in the ammonium phosphate to a range of relatively low solubility and therefore the slurry solidifies immediately on the surface of the recycled fines. Excess ammonia is used to force the reaction to go to the diammonium phosphate ratio; the excess escapes and is caught in the same scrubber that handles gas from the preneutralizer.

The resulting 18-46-0 product has become one of the most popular "chemically mixed" materials. It is simple and easy to make, units can be built large enough to make 50 tons or more per hour, and the high concentration gives an important shipping and handling advantage. Many large DAP plants were built in the latter part of the 1960–1970 decade, particularly in Florida where high concentration is especially important because any fertilizer product must be shipped a long way to market (mainly to the Midwest).

But even though straight diammonium phosphate is probably the most important of the various ammonium phosphate-type products, others have also gained a significant place in the industry. In the United States, for example, a combination of ammonium sulfate and ammonium phosphate is popular; grades such as 16-20-0 and 13-13-13 are typical. This allows making a product with higher nitrogen-to-phosphate ratio for farming situations that require it. The mixture is easy to make, by using some sulfuric acid along with the phosphoric. In the United Kingdom, on the other hand, a combination of ammonium phosphate and ammonium nitrate is widely used. The ammonium nitrate serves the same purpose as the ammonium sulfate in the United States practice but does not reduce the grade so much; for example, a 16-16-16 can be made. Moreover, the presence of the ammonium nitrate makes it possible to prill the mix because the molten ammonium nitrate (after evaporation) carries the ammonium phosphate along as a solution or slurry that is fluid enough to be sprayed into the prilling tower, an operation that is infeasible with ammonium sulfate-phosphate. Prilling is generally regarded as less expensive than rotary-drum granulation and the product spheres are more attractive than granules with their sometimes irregular shape.

The latest combination is urea with ammonium phosphate, a product that is somewhat difficult to make because the urea is sensitive to heat and acidity and thus may decompose to some extent during neutralization and drying. However, the grade is quite high (typically 18-18-18), as high as can be obtained with the materials in commercial use. A plant has been built recently in India and fertilizer producers have shown much interest in the material. Research is under way on methods for granulating with minimum urea decomposition.

The ammonium phosphates, diammonium phosphate in particular, are very good fertilizers; they are highly concentrated, of good physical condition, and economical to make. Nevertheless, research and development people have not been satisfied. Research goes on to improve properties and push concentration even higher. The newest entry in the race is ammonium polyphosphate, made by reacting ammonia with polyphosphoric acid (the superphosphoric that we discussed earlier) rather than ordinary phosphoric acid. The over-all concentration is not increased very much because the only gain is from water driven out of the phosphate molecules in making the chain-type acids; the grades range from 12-58-0 to 15-60-0 (total of 60-75) as compared with a range of 11-48-0 to 21-54-0 (total of 59-75) in the usual procedure. However, the phosphate content is higher, and this is desirable for products made in Florida because phosphate is the important consideration, not nitrogen. Moreover, the polyphosphate has a special property, which we will discuss later, that ordinary phosphate does not have.

Ammonium polyphosphate has been a challenge to the chemical engineers because the production situation is entirely different from ordinary ammonium phosphate. Polyphosphoric acid contains no water, so there is no need for a dryer or for any arrangement to use reaction heat for boiling out water during the ammoniation step. When the acid is ammoniated, the high heat of reaction melts the product (because of chemical differences it is easier to melt than ammonium phosphate made by the usual method). With a dry melt made this easily, the logical course is prilling. But unfortunately the melt is a viscous, sticky liquid that crystallizes very slowly when cooled; if it were sprayed into a prilling tower, the drops would not crystallize and harden rapidly during the fall as ammonium nitrate or urea do, but would flatten out on striking the tower floor and probably stick together.

Such a viscous liquid can often be crystallized and hardened by putting energy into it, or, in process terms, "working" it. The engineers have found that this works well for ammonium polyphosphate. The granulating device used is a paddle mixer (or pug mill), a trough-like device with heavy paddles mounted on a shaft turning lengthwise in it. Recycled fines are fed into the mixer along with melt from the ammoniator; the paddles mix and churn the two until granulation takes place; and the working makes the melt crystallize.

This is a good process if furnace-type superphosphoric acid is used because the equipment needed—reactor, pug mill, and screens—is less complex than that required for making ammonium phosphate by the usual route. But when wet-process acid is the choice, then the step of converting ordinary acid to the super type, by boiling out water and heating further to dehydrate the phosphate, adds expense. It does not make economic sense to first supply heat to boil out water and then use cooling water to remove the large amount of heat evolved during ammoniation.

So why not do both jobs and use the reaction heat to remove the water? This has worked quite well. [Here we are on the research frontier, for at this writing (1969) the so-called "direct" method is still under development.] Ordinary wet-process acid (54 percent P_2O_5) is fed to a series of reactors in which the acid flows one way and ammonia the other. The reactors are insulated to conserve heat and to allow development of a temperature high enough to boil all the water out and also dehydrate the phosphate. The product melt of ammonium polyphosphate is granulated in a pug mill in the same way as just described.

Ammonium polyphosphate is not yet produced commercially. It is too new. But its superior properties are likely to make it an important fertilizer in the future.

Why Not Use Nitric Acid?

A very strong acid is required to dissolve phosphate rock and convert it to phosphoric acid; if the acid is not stronger than the phosphoric acid it cannot very well do the job. So far the only acid we have mentioned that is strong enough for this is sulfuric acid, the most powerful of all the common acids. Another candidate is nitric acid, which is not as strong as sulfuric but still quite able to dissolve phosphate rock.

Why is nitric acid not always preferred over sulfuric, since the nitrate part of nitric acid is a good fertilizer material whereas the sulfate in sulfuric either dilutes the phosphate (in superphosphate) or must be thrown away (in making phosphoric acid)? The equation for the reaction tells the story.

$$[Ca_3(PO_4)_2]_3\,CaF_2 \;+\; 20HNO_3 \longrightarrow$$

phosphate rock   nitric acid

$$6H_3PO_4 \;+\; 10Ca(NO_3)_2 + 2HF\uparrow$$

phosphoric   calcium
acid   nitrate

Here the calcium compound formed is calcium nitrate rather than calcium sulfate and this is the problem. The calcium nitrate is a very troublesome product, difficult to handle any way we go about it. When we use sulfuric acid the calcium sulfate formed is easy to separate because it is not soluble in the phosphoric acid and we can filter it out. But calcium nitrate is quite soluble so we must find some other way to make the separation.

But why not leave it in, ammoniate the acid to make ammonium phosphate, and end up with a mixed product? This is what happens.

$$6H_3PO_4 + 10Ca(NO_3)_2 + 20NH_3 + 2H_2O \longrightarrow$$

$$\underset{\substack{\text{ammonium} \\ \text{nitrate}}}{20NH_4NO_3} + \underset{\substack{\text{apatite}}}{[Ca_3(PO_4)_2]_3Ca(OH)_2}$$

Now we are in trouble because the apatite formed is a very insoluble material, not so inert as the original phosphate rock but still not soluble enough to be a fully satisfactory fertilizer.

Perhaps if we did not use so much ammonia we could do better.

$$6H_3PO_4 + 10Ca(NO_3)_2 + 12NH_3 \longrightarrow$$

$$\underset{\substack{\text{ammonium} \\ \text{nitrate}}}{12NH_4NO_3} + \underset{\substack{\text{dicalcium} \\ \text{phosphate}}}{6CaHPO_4} + \underset{\substack{\text{calcium} \\ \text{nitrate}}}{4Ca(NO_3)_2}$$

This looks like the way to go, for the dicalcium phosphate, although not soluble in water, is an acceptable fertilizer. But even though the phosphoric acid is all neutralized, we still have a good part of the calcium nitrate unreacted —the excess over that converted to dicalcium phosphate. Ordinarily this would not hurt anything but remember that calcium nitrate is a bad actor in many ways; the trouble here is that it is so thirsty and hygroscopic it cannot be tolerated in a mixed fertilizer. It is even worse than ammonium nitrate, which is pretty bad, and when they are together as in this reaction product the mix would pick up water in a desert.

So we must look elsewhere for a solution to the problem. Perhaps we could use just enough of some other acid to tie up the excess calcium nitrate.

$$6H_3PO_4 + 10Ca(NO_3)_2 + 4H_3PO_4 + 20NH_3 \longrightarrow$$
$$20NH_4NO_3 + 10CaHPO_4$$

Now we have it. The calcium nitrate is gone, the product has good physical condition, and we have a good fertilizer mixture. In effect we have made ammonium nitrate from nitric acid and ammonia, just as if we had started out to do that in the first place, but along the way we stopped and put the nitric acid to work dissolving phosphate rock. This is equivalent to getting the rock acidulation free, whereas if we use sulfuric acid all the cost of the acid must be charged to the acidulation step and the sulfate must be discarded after the rock has been dissolved.

The good economics of using nitric acid in this way has made nitric phosphate a popular fertilizer in some parts of the world, particularly in Europe. But in practice it is not made exactly like the last equation shows. Although the dicalcium phosphate is generally regarded as a good fertilizer its lack of water solubility makes it a little on the slow side in crop response. (Remember the general discussion of the pros and cons of water solubility in Chap. 2.) To avoid this, most producers use more phosphoric acid than the equation indicates.

$$6H_3PO_4 + 10Ca(NO_3)_2 + 11H_3PO_4 + 27NH_3 \longrightarrow$$
$$20NH_4NO_2 + 10CaHPO_4 + 7NH_4H_2PO_4$$
monoammonium
phosphate

Now a little over 40 percent of the phosphate is present as ammonium phosphate, a completely water-soluble material. This degree of water solubility is generally regarded as satisfactory.

But we have used so much phosphoric acid that instead of a nitric phosphate process we have a nitric phosphate-ammonium phosphate process. Moreover, one of the main advantages of nitric phosphate production has been partially lost. We have seen earlier how the phosphate industry has been hit hard by the shortage of sulfur for making the sulfuric acid needed in phosphoric acid production. By shifting to nitric acid we eliminate the need for sulfuric acid in dissolving the phosphate rock, but if we use enough phosphoric acid to get 40 percent water solubility then we have to have about 60 percent as much sulfuric as would have been needed if we had followed the ammonium phosphate route in the first place and forgotten about using nitric acid.

This sad state of affairs has led researchers to seek still other ways of getting around the calcium nitrate problem and at the same time getting some water solubility. The search has been successful but it has been a difficult road, very much in keeping with the many other difficult but important developments that have made the fertilizer industry highly efficient and economical and have pushed it to a high level of importance in the field of chemistry and chemical engineering. The result of this search was the Odda process, which got its name from the town in Norway where it started.

Since calcium nitrate is so troublesome, the Odda researchers looked for ways to separate it, or at least part of it, from the phosphoric acid. As we said earlier, this is not easy because the calcium nitrate is soluble. But it can be done by cooling the product solution down to such a low temperature that the calcium nitrate freezes (crystallizes) out.

There were many problems. Crystals were hard to grow to a size large enough for good separation (by filtering or centrifuging), impurities from the phosphate rock interfered with filtration, washing the calcium nitrate to prevent phosphate loss was difficult, and so on. By application of a considerable amount of engineering ingenuity these problems were solved and today the Odda process is the usual choice for new plants.

The operation goes like this

I. $6H_3PO_4 + 10Ca(NO_3)_2 \xrightarrow{\text{cooling}}$
$6H_3PO_4 + 3.5Ca(NO_3)_2 + 6.5Ca(NO_3)_2 \downarrow$

II. $6H_3PO_4 + 3.5Ca(NO_3)_2 + 9.5NH_3 \longrightarrow$
$7NH_4NO_3 + 3.5CaHPO_4 + 2.5NH_4H_2PO_4$

So by freezing out 65 percent of the calcium nitrate, we get a product with the desired 40 percent water solubility but without using any phosphoric acid at all.

Most of the process steps are like those in production of phosphoric acid and ammonium phosphate. Phosphate rock is dissolved with nitric acid in a tank, the slurry is pumped to another tank where refrigerant circulating through coils brings the temperature down to the proper level, the crystals that form are separated by centrifuging or filtering, and the crystal-free solution is ammoniated and granulated in the same way as in ammonium phosphate production. Grades such as 23-23-0 and 17-17-17 are made.

But what to do with the calcium nitrate left over? Fortunately, it is not so thirsty when alone rather than mixed with ammonium nitrate, so much of it is used as such in Europe; bags of good quality are used to prevent or delay moisture absorption. Another method is to convert it to ammonium nitrate.

$$Ca(NO_3)_2 + 2NH_3 + CO_2 + H_2O \longrightarrow$$

$$2NH_4NO_3 + CaCO_3 \downarrow$$

calcium
carbonate

The calcium carbonate is insoluble and can be separated by filtration. The ammonium nitrate solution is concentrated by evaporation and prilled. As in urea production, this method is feasible only when an ammonia plant is operated nearby and the waste carbon dioxide piped from it to the calcium nitrate conversion unit.

Nitric phosphate has become a major fertilizer in Europe, where in the past most of the sulfur had to be imported. In the United States, however, cheap sulfur and the entrenched position of superphosphate and ammonium phosphate have pretty well kept nitric phosphate out. This situation may well change if sulfur continues to be scarce and high priced. There are now over fifty nitric phosphate plants throughout the world, producing a significant part of world fertilizer phosphate.

The technology has been well developed, to the point that nitric phosphate economics, particularly for the Odda process, compare well with other processes. But the search for a better process goes on. One of the main problems still unsolved is that a lot of ammonium nitrate must be made along with the phosphate. This may not always be the economical thing to do; in Florida, for example, phosphate production is the major objective and ammonium nitrate is best made somewhere else. One way to avoid this would be to separate the calcium nitrate, decompose it to nitric acid and lime, and recycle the nitric acid. Such a process shows promise of being an engineering nightmare, but then researchers such as Haber and his many successors never let such petty annoyances bother them in the past. As would be expected, then, research on calcium nitrate decomposition is proceeding.

Fertilizer We Can Pump

Most people are lazy and farmers are no exception. Lifting bags of fertilizer and emptying them into a spreader is hard work. But the farmer, and the dealer who supplies him, are also good businessmen. If there is some way of reducing the labor required for handling fertilizer, labor that gets scarcer and more costly every year, they are all for it.

One of the answers to the labor problem is liquid fertilizer, fertilizer that flows through pipes and pumps without ever requiring any manual labor for lifting at all. All we need is a tank installation for making it, tank trucks for transporting it, a tank-equipped spreader for spraying it on the soil, and pumps to transfer it from one piece of equipment to another.

Liquid fertilizer is a new type—not that it wasn't known in the past for it was mentioned in accounts of fertilizer practice over a hundred years ago. But commercial significance began late, in the early 1950s, after all the other major fertilizers were fairly well established. The first liquid mixed fertilizer plant east of the Rockies started up in 1954.

Making liquid fertilizer requires materials that will dissolve in water, of course, and fortunately many of the fertilizers we have met earlier meet this requirement. But one of the drawbacks is that the water used to dissolve the nutrient compounds lowers the product grade. So we must use the most concentrated materials to offset the diluting effect of the water. These are ammonium nitrate and urea for supplying nitrogen, ammonium phosphate for phosphate, and potassium chloride for potash. Some of the older materials, such as sodium nitrate, ammonium sulfate, and superphosphate have no place in the new liquid technology.

Liquid fertilizers have been a challenge to the technologists, particularly to the chemists, because of the complicated solubility relationships involved. We saw earlier how the chemists solved the problem of crystallizing out the various materials, including potassium chloride, from lake brines. Making liquid fertilizers presents the same kind of problem except in reverse; the job with the brines was to crystallize out the dissolved compounds cleanly, without getting one contaminated with the other; the job with liquid fertilizers is getting the materials into solution in such a way that they won't crystallize out at all.

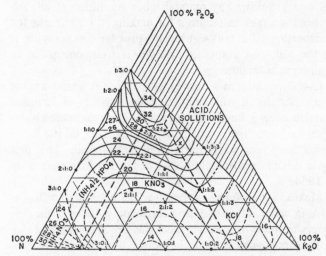

Fig. 10 This does not look like a map, but it is one nevertheless—a map of solubilities that the liquid fertilizer producer must have.

This requires a detailed knowledge of how the proportions between the materials affect overall solubility—

knowledge that no one had when the liquid fertilizer industry began. So the chemists went to work and measured the solubility over a wide range of ratios between materials. Then they drew a map (called a triangular solubility diagram) so that producers could figure out how much water to use in making a solution of given nutrient ratio. The amount of water is very important; the lower the amount used the higher will be the concentration of the product, but if too little is used the fertilizer will salt out (crystallize). Any such salting out is quite troublesome because the crystals clog lines, tanks, and spreading equipment.

We can illustrate the problem by a typical formulation (proportioning) situation. Suppose we want to make a grade of 1:1:1 ratio, meaning that we will have equal weights of nitrogen (N), phosphate (P_2O_5), and potash (K_2O). We have on hand urea, ammonium phosphate, and potassium chloride. It is easy to calculate how much of each to use to get our 1:1:1, but how much water shall we add? It might be said that we should use just enough to dissolve the mix. But suppose it is springtime, the main season for making fertilizer, and the weather is warm. Then we had better use more water than this, because if the weather turns cold our dissolved materials will crystallize right back out again and the customer will be most unhappy. So we go to the solubility map (Fig. 10) the chemists have provided us, a map that tells us how much water to use to keep the solution from crystallizing until the temperature has gotten down to 32° F., the freezing point of water, which is generally regarded as being as low a temperature as we need to worry about (with some exceptions, depending on what part of the country we are in and what season of the year it is). The map has three corners, one corner for 100 percent N, one for 100 percent P_2O_5, and the third for 100 percent K_2O. Points inside the map, then, give us various ratios between the three.

And over the map go meandering lines, each of which represents a certain total nutrient content that is stable at 32° F. All we have to do is locate our ratio and then note which of the nutrient content lines is nearest to it. In our case, the 1:1:1 ratio will be at the center of the diagram and the nearest concentration line says 22 percent, which means that we must add enough water to the mix to give a total nutrient concentration of 22 percent; the resulting grade for a 1:1:1 ratio, of course, is 7-7-7 (nearest whole number ratio).

The first thing to consider in making a liquid fertilizer is how to proportion the ammonia and phosphoric acid in the ammonium phosphate. As we saw earlier in the description of ammonium phosphate production, about two parts of monoammonium phosphate ($NH_4H_2PO_4$) to one of diammonium phosphate [$(NH_4)_2HPO_4$] gives the highest solubility. This is the ratio used in the liquid fertilizer industry.

Actually, liquid fertilizers are seldom made from solid materials; they cost too much. The standard practice is to react ammonia with phosphoric acid and then add the other constituents. Only the potash is added as a solid, and this would not be done if a liquid form of potash were available. The nitrogen comes in as a solution of urea and ammonium nitrate, which are used together because of the high mutual solubility effect (meaning that together they are much more soluble than either is alone). When the two are properly proportioned the solution can hold 32 percent nitrogen without salting out until the temperature is below freezing; for either of them used alone, only about 20 percent nitrogen will stay in solution at this temperature.

The chemists have been hard at work trying to improve liquid fertilizers ever since farmers started using them. An improvement obviously needed was some way to get the concentration higher without getting into salting-out trouble.

The improvement came right along when the chemists and engineers put their minds to it. Instead of using ordinary phosphoric acid, they turned to the superphosphoric acid that we have met earlier. Ammonia and superphosphoric acid gives ammonium polyphosphate, as we have seen, and the ammonium polyphosphate is much more soluble than ordinary ammonium phosphate. Instead of 8-24-0, a popular grade made from ordinary acid, 11-37-0 can be made from superphosphoric acid. The 11-37-0 has become a very popular material in the liquid fertilizer industry.

Another problem was in using wet-process phosphoric acid. "Wet acid" contains impurities dissolved from the original phosphate rock, and some of them, particularly iron and aluminum compounds, come out of solution as a bulky mass of solids when the acid is ammoniated.

Why would anyone want to use such a troublesome raw material when superphosphoric acid does so much better? The trouble is that super acid costs more than the ordinary wet acid, and therefore the producer would like to use as much of the wet acid as he can.

Super acid came to the rescue in this problem also, but in a different way entirely. It had been known for a long time in the chemical industry that polyphosphates are good to use in boiler water treatment to prevent scale formation and in soaps and detergents to improve their dirt-removing ability. What the polyphosphate in these products does, in a chemical way, is to sequester materials that cause the boiler scale or the ring in the bathtub. "Sequester" is a word that ordinarily means to set apart or separate, but in chemistry it means to hold something in solution that otherwise would come out.

The chemists looked at ammonium polyphosphate and

wondered if it would sequester like the sodium and potassium polyphosphates in detergents do. When they tried it on the impurities in wet-process phosphoric acid, it worked very well, holding the iron and aluminum in solution and giving a clear product rather than the dirty, solids-laden liquid formed when wet acid is ammoniated without any additive.

Using super acid (or 11-37-0) for sequestering impurities is now an established practice. By supplying from 10 to 30 percent of the phosphate as super acid and the remainder as ordinary wet acid, a solids-free product can be made without greatly increasing the cost.

The latest departure in the liquid fertilizer field is a product called "suspension fertilizer." It is the result of a compromise—a marrying of solid and liquid fertilizers in an attempt to get most of the advantages of each with a minimum of the disadvantages. The product in effect is a salted-out liquid fertilizer, for in making the suspension the amount of water used is purposely cut down to the point that all the nutrient compounds cannot be held in solution and crystallization therefore occurs.

This, you may say, is just what we warned against in making liquid fertilizers because the crystals clog equipment. That is correct; the difference is that in making the suspensions the crystals are kept small by special techniques, a suspending agent (usually a gelling type of clay) is used to minimize settling in tanks, and special equipment is used in handling and in spreading on the farm.

By going the suspension route, we get around several of the drawbacks in making and using liquid fertilizer: salting out is not a problem because the product is already salted out, and the grade is much higher, as high, in fact, as most solid fertilizers. For example, a 15-15-15 suspension can be made as compared with the limit of 9-9-9 for the clear liquid type. So the suspension has the high-analysis advantage of solid fertilizers but does not cake and is less expensive, in most instances, to produce. And it can be pumped and handled economically like clear liquids but salting out is not a problem.

Offsetting these outstanding good points is the radically different nature of suspensions; they are different in appearance and in the techniques required for storage, handling, and application. Farmers therefore have been slow to accept them because farmers are mainly a conservative lot. The practice is growing, however, and it is expected to grow faster in the future. The favorable economics are there and in time this should be the deciding consideration.

An Old Practice Returns

As we have seen earlier, in the beginning decades of the fertilizer industry mixed fertilizers were mainly simple dry mixtures of materials, usually ammonium sulfate, sodium nitrate, superphosphate, and potassium chloride. As no effort was made to granulate, the product was mostly a mixture of dust and lumps, quite unattractive in comparison to a closely sized modern material such as prilled ammonium nitrate or granulated diammonium phosphate. Also, the mix was generally sold in bags, because bulk handling had not been developed very far in those days.

With the advent of granular fertilizers made from ammoniated superphosphate, the nongranular simple mixed fertilizers fell rapidly into disfavor. And granular diammonium phosphate was another major blow. The practice of dry mixing fertilizers seemed on the way out.

But then came the beginnings, in about the middle of the 1950–60 decade, of a new practice called "bulk blending." The name did not distinguish it very much for "blending" was just another word for mixing. And that is what it was; the fertilizer industry had gone full cycle and had returned to the old dry mixing of fifty years past. The bulk blend plants were simple mixing operations and the plants were small, just as were the old dry mix plants.

But there were some important differences. One was the use of granular materials only, as compared with the powders of the past. Another was the high analysis, because only high-grade materials were used in the blend (ammonium nitrate, urea, triple superphosphate, DAP, and potassium chloride) and, finally, the product was handled and applied in bulk to avoid the cost of bagging.

The real basis for bringing the old practice back was that the good points of dry mixing—low equipment cost (low investment), small sales area, and direct contact with the customer—are just as important today as they ever were. The granulation plants have to be fairly large because of the high investment; a small granulation plant would have much too high an investment per ton of product. But blending (or mixing) is such a simple operation that investment per unit of product is quite low even in a small plant. Furthermore, because of the small production the blend does not have to be shipped as far (on the average) and therefore there is less freight to pay. And finally, the direct contact with the farmer (because the plants are small, usually serving only one community each) helps in selling the fertilizer.

Equipment needs for bulk blending are simple: storage buildings or silos for the materials, a weighing system, and a mixer (usually of the cement-mixer type). It is quite common for the blender to mix to order and discharge directly into a truck that carries the fertilizer to the farm. The truck is equipped with a spreader fan (fan at the back that throws the fertilizer granules out in a wide swath as the truck is driven along over the field), so no transfer to other equipment at the farm is required. Such a system is one of the most economical ways of getting a mixed fertilizer produced and applied to the soil.

Bulk blending grew with amazing rapidity in the 1955–65 decade; at the last count there were well over 1500 plants in the United States. The method is not as economical in other countries where the materials cost situation is different.

It costs very little, relatively speaking, to get into the bulk blend business and this has been one of its main attractions. In almost every community there was someone who could raise enough capital to get into the fertilizer business by this low-cost route. And once established it was hard for the large granulating producers to compete with him. In self defense, many of the large producers went into the bulk blending business themselves, setting up small blending plants in various communities and shipping to them materials made in the company's large central plants.

Bulk blending is expected to grow in the future, perhaps not so much because of economics but because it fits in with the concept of a community service center for the farmer. The modern farmer operates a complicated business and needs many types of services. A local service center can test his soil, mix fertilizers to his particular need, supply pesticides to protect his crops, and generally serve as the bridge between modern chemical technology and the farm. The main threat to bulk blending in this system is liquid mixed fertilizer, which as we have seen is also a simple, economical mixing operation carried out in small, community-sized plants.

Chapter 8

Food for the Future

We have seen that the past fifty years has brought into being a new fertilizer industry, little related to the older and simpler practice but instead a major newcomer to chemical engineering technology. What will the next fifty years bring? Will the industry continue to change at the rapid rate we have become accustomed to? And are there problems on the horizon that will be more difficult than those of the past?

We shall examine the future under several different categories—from the viewpoints both of fertilizer production technology and of food production in general.

New Fertilizers

One of the trends that is easy to see is a growing adoption of the fluid fertilizers—anhydrous ammonia, nitrogen solutions, and liquid mixed fertilizers. As man increases mastery of his environment, and thus increases his standard of living, time becomes more and more precious. The man-hours saved by fertilizers that can be pumped will be even more important in the future than they are today.

The main changes will be to new types of fluid fertilizers that have higher nutrient concentration and superior handling qualities. Suspensions should move forward particularly, and liquid mixed fertilizers based on potassium polyphosphate (very high concentration) may reach the point of being economical.

Higher concentration in solid fertilizers may also come, although urea, ammonium phosphate, and potassium chloride, the present standard high-analysis materials, are very highly concentrated themselves. Research is under way on fertilizers made by combining phosphorus, ammonia, and air in a gas phase reaction at high temperature. The products are so complicated chemically that they have defied analysis so far, but they are very high-analysis materials indeed. Some of them run over 100 percent nutrient, for example, 15-90-0—offhand a quite impossible feat. But as we have seen earlier, the antiquated oxide basis for reporting phosphorus and potash content makes such a thing possible. On any basis, however, the phosphorus-ammonia-oxygen products are very highly concentrated and should become important fertilizer materials if production problems can be worked out.

The term "tailored-release" may be part of the future fertilizer terminology. As we have seen, sulfur coatings on nitrogen fertilizers have been developed to the point that they give slow and uniform nitrogen release in the soil— and at a cost low enough to make coated fertilizers acceptable from the economic standpoint. It may be possible to carry this technique further and make fertilizers that release nutrient at just the rate the plant needs it, a goal that agronomists have had for a long time. The tailored-release fertilizer would supply a limited amount of nutrient when the plant was young, larger amounts during the later stages of growth, and special boosts during those periods of the plant's life when its needs were the greatest.

Moreover, the coating technique may make it possible to "store" fertilizers on or in the farmer's fields rather than in expensive storage buildings. An annual application, made during the winter when more time is available than during the busy spring planting season, may be adequate. Hopefully, the fertilizer would lie there inert, just as if it were in conventional storage, and then become available as the weather warmed up and the microbial life in the soil became active again.

Many other developments are in the offing—better

physical condition, more streamlined processes, lower production labor requirement, better utilization of by-products, reduced material losses—advancements that may not be as interesting as the ones mentioned earlier but which are nevertheless very important in reducing the cost of plant nutrients to the farmer. All of them point to a highly advanced fertilizer industry in the future, geared to an equally advanced technology of food production.

The Impact of Nuclear Power

One of the greatest advancements ever made in chemistry and physics took place in the 1930s when the first nuclear fission reaction was carried out. Man had at last tapped into the vast reservoirs of energy stored up in the atom, energy of an intensity undreamed of before. Since then the less interesting but highly important business of working out the technology has been going forward, step by step and disappointment by disappointment as is usual for new technologies.

The role of nuclear energy in warfare is well known. But hopefully the impact on power production will be far more important in the history of mankind, for our power is produced mainly in gigantic plants that swallow trainloads of coal or oil each day. We have been fortunate in the great fossil deposits that give us, for our day, a cheap and plentiful source of fuel. But just as for phosphate and potash, our children's children's children will not have nearly so much and some day they will not have any at all.

The development of nuclear power shifts the load from the fossil fuels to uranium, which may not appear to be a great advance, for uranium reserves are limited too. But another development, coming along fast, is a device called a "breeder" reactor that makes about as much nuclear fuel as it consumes. When this is fully developed and adopted, which should be in the 1970s or 1980s, the nuclear fuel supply will be assured for a long time to come.

But how does all this affect fertilizer production? Simply because the fertilizer industry is a large consumer of energy also, just as are power plants. The main raw material in making ammonia is natural gas and this gives up its energy in the process, not by burning as coal and oil do in the power plant but by chemical reactions that accomplish the same thing, for the end product in both power plant and the ammonia plant is carbon dioxide.

And in phosphate production sulfur is also a supplier of energy, for it starts in the elemental form, the highest energy level, and ends as calcium sulfate, a very low energy level indeed.

Nuclear power can replace both these sources. Instead of the gas or oil or coal, that react with water to give the hydrogen needed for ammonia, the electric power from nuclear plants can electrolyze water to give hydrogen directly and also oxygen as a bonus byproduct. Thus, in effect, the nuclear fuel takes the place of fossil fuel, but with the advantage that very little nuclear fuel is required.

We have already covered the role of electric power in breaking down phosphate ore to make phosphorus. Here the coal or oil used in making the power, plus the coke and silica that react with the phosphate, take the place of the sulfur in the wet process. Nuclear power mainly eliminates the fossil fuel requirement in making power, as we have seen, so that a relatively small amount of coke, plus silica which is plentiful, do the same job as the sulfur. And since sulfur is rapidly becoming more expensive to win from the earth, nuclear power may become an important contributor to the phosphate industry.

If we had to wait until we ran out of coal and oil before nuclear power became important, there would not be much point in talking about it here. But it is already important for another reason: at many places the nuclear route is cheaper. One of the largest power producers in the world, the Tennessee Valley Authority, has found that the economics tip to nuclear even in a region where coal can be mined by surface stripping, at relatively low cost. By 1975 TVA plans to have several very large power boilers built and operating on nuclear fuel. Throughout the power industry the same trend is taking place, an ever-accelerating shift from combustion to nuclear fission.

A revolutionary and daring concept for use of nuclear power is being studied by the Atomic Energy Commission. A tremendous nuclear power plant would be built at some appropriate site, with the large size aimed at getting low power cost. At the same time, industries of the type that require large amounts of power would be built near the power plant, because the amount of power produced would be too large for an ordinary industrial situation (and the cost of transmitting for a long distance over power lines would be too high). And integrated into this power industry complex would be use of waste heat from the power plant to remove the salt from ocean water, thus getting rid of two problems at once: the growing shortage of clean fresh water for industrial use and the "thermal pollution" that the waste heat produces when water from lakes or running streams is used to cool the power plant condensers.

The fertilizer industry comes into this scheme because ammonia and phosphorus production are two of the most appropriate heavy power consumers that could be selected. Such a complex, with ammonia and phosphorus integrated into it, could be a major contributor to supplying the fertilizer needed in developing countries where the raw materials we take for granted, such as water, are often in short supply.

The Sulfur Problem

The shortage of sulfur that plagued the fertilizer industry in the latter part of the 1960s is, to some extent, a recurring thing. As for any basic commodity, there is a tendency for the industry to build new supply facilities when the price is high and then to stop building when oversupply brings the price back down again. This has happened repeatedly, in a sort of sine-wave cycle, over the history of the sulfur industry, and very likely will happen again. So the sulfur supply situation may return to one of plenty rather than shortage.

But as we have seen, the future will bring a new problem, that of accelerating exhaustion of the low-cost Frasch sulfur reserves. New sources must be found, and the finding of these will be one of the major development efforts in the future of the fertilizer industry.

New Ways of Farming

So far, in trying to predict the future, we have considered how to make better fertilizer and how to make enough fertilizer. But there is an end to what fertilizer can do to increase food production. When the land has been put into good physical condition, the crop planted as closely as is feasible (to get the optimum number of plants per acre for maximum production), and fertilizer applied in an amount high enough to keep plant nutrient supply from being a limiting factor, then the fertilizer producer and the farmer have done all that they can do. When the time comes that this is not enough to feed the world, some other way to increase food production must be found.

Here we leave the area of fertilizer technology and move into the realm of the plant breeder, the agricultural economist, the nutritionist, and many others who play important parts in the overall subject of human nutrition. All of these areas of effort tie together, however, and we must consider them all in looking into the future of fertilizers.

The plant breeders are making very important contributions. We can only touch on this extensive subject here. It is enough to say that new varieties of food plants have been developed which bear a much greater food load (usually seeds) per plant and which have strong enough stalks to support it. This last is very important, for it does no good to develop a plant that bears heavily if the plant structure gives way under the weight before harvest time. A good example of this is a new variety of wheat that has short, strong stalks and a large seed head; this particular variety is even now increasing food production in countries such as India. The plant breeders also develop plant varieties that are more concentrated in human nutrient, thus in effect increasing yield per acre.

Other scientists and technologists help with such problems as getting rid of the pests and diseases that keep plants from reaching maximum growth. Others attack the water problem, a very important one because all efforts are useless unless the plant gets enough water and unless the water is fed to it at the proper rate (not too little or too much at any one growth period).

All this affects the fertilizers of the future because with continued advancement in these allied fields, special fertilizers and special methods of application may well be needed.

But now let us look at the time when all these technologists have done their utmost—fertilizers have become very highly concentrated, economical, and tailored to the situation; the plant has been bred to maximum growth potential and food value; the environment has been controlled to avoid any interference with growth; and the farmer has prepared the soil well and planted thick enough to give the plant population optimum for yield per acre. But the population has increased to the point that all this is not enough. What do we do?

By that time, bringing new acres into production will not be the answer for all arable land will have been converted to crop growth long before. We will have lost ground probably from the inroads of parks, golf courses, cities, highways, airports, and industry. Some land can be reclaimed from the sea by diking off shallow areas, but even this probably will already have been exploited.

No more land and no more hope of more food per acre. Then must come the painful consideration of changing the type of crop to get higher production, a course that people have generally resisted because they like certain foods and don't want to change to something else. In the United States we like a lot of milk and eggs, in Argentina people eat more beef than in other parts of the world, in the Orient rice is the preferred food, and so on. But the favorite food in a given country may not be the one that gives the highest yield per acre.

This problem comes mainly in the growing of protein, which in most countries requires the growing of animals, such as cattle, sheep, poultry, to get the protein that people like. Unfortunately, the growing of animals is a very inefficient way of using land for food production because the land must be used to grow food for the animal which in turn becomes the food for man. There is so much lost motion in this that the equivalent yield of meat per acre is relatively low. It would be much better to grow a high-protein plant and use it directly as food.

There are several plants, soybeans and cotton (the seeds) for example, that are very good sources of protein. Cotton seeds give a meal that contains up to 50 percent protein, at a cost far lower and a yield much higher than for protein from cattle or sheep. But who would settle for soybeans or cottonseed meal when he wants steak?

This aversion to plant proteins, which are just as nutritious as animal proteins, is a current problem in efforts to improve the diet of people in the underdeveloped countries of the world. Most of these people do not get enough protein because they can't afford meat. They could afford, in many cases at least, a combination of one-third soybean flour and two-thirds flour or cornmeal, which contains over 25 percent protein and is roughly equivalent in food value to meat, milk, or eggs. But they won't eat it. Or at least it is hard to get them to eat it. The situation seems to be something like that in dog foods; one can of dog food, made up of vegetable oils and cereals, may be just as high in protein and just as nutritious as another based on horse meat (and much cheaper). But the dog prefers the horse meat.

Some progress has been made in improving palatability of the vegetable proteins. A mixture called Incaparina is being used more and more in Central and South America; one pound of Incaparina is equivalent in protein content to about twenty eggs. Peanut flour is being used in India and soy flour in South Africa and Argentina.

A unique way of getting people to accept vegetable protein is a venture of the drink companies in which the protein is incorporated in a tastefully flavored soft drink. Since the children suffer especially from protein deficiency, it is hoped that the soft drink route will be an effective way to get them to accept a protein supplement.

The substitution of vegetable for animal protein probably will never be complete, because the well-to-do will pay the extra price for meat. But if a substantial part of the protein requirement can be shifted away from the animal type, much more food can be produced on the available land and at a price more in line with what the less affluent people can afford to pay. With improved plant varieties and heavy use of fertilizer, bumper crops of the equivalent of meat, milk, and eggs can be produced per acre.

Farther out in the future is the possibility of converting the vegetable protein to something that tastes like animal products. Already the protein from soybeans has been isolated, purified, and converted to products with the texture of meat. The similated "hamburgers," "ham," and "fish" are said to be quite palatable but currently are too expensive.

Food from the Sea

Man long ago exhausted the protein resources of field and forest. He continues to hunt the animals he once depended on as a major part of his food, but today it is for sport and if he eats the game it is a novelty rather than a standard item for the table.

This is not true of the sea. Man has taken over the land, occupying almost every square mile and steadily reducing it to a place unsuitable and inhospitable to wild animal life. But he has never taken over the sea. It is inhospitable to man and protects its own within its deeps. There is no way to take a census of marine life, but it seems unlikely that the activities of man, restricted as they are mainly to the land, have had much effect on the populations of the sea. In contrast, most land animals have declined in number, some almost to extinction.

The teeming life in the oceans has always been a source of food for man and continues to be so. In fact, world production of marine fish has increased rapidly since 1950. In Peru, for example, fish production increased from 50,000 tons in 1954 to about 9,000,000 tons in 1964.

Here we leave fertilizer technology behind. We cannot fertilize an acre of ocean as we do an acre of land, and if we did the fish we hope to grow would not stay put as do cattle in a fertilized pasture. The sea is wild and so are the creatures in it. There have been efforts at fencing off shallow inlets and growing captive fish or other marine life in them, with fertilization to increase growth of marine plants on which the fish feed, and this may have promise for the future. The main practice for some time to come, however, will be fishing in the open sea.

The sea should supply more and more of man's food in the future. With improved methods of locating and catching fish, it should be possible to expand production without overharvesting. The sea would be a more important source of food now if it were not for the cost of catching and processing the fish, particularly the latter. The most economical method is to grind up the entire catch without any effort to remove portions ordinarily regarded as inedible; with proper processing the product is quite sanitary and nutritious. In fact, large quantities of fish meal are used in animal and poultry feeds. The ordinary fish meal, however, is so smelly and bad tasting that it is quite unacceptable as human food (remember cod liver oil). Processes have been developed for removing the taste and odor, giving a product acceptable for human consumption from this standpoint, but the esthetic resistance to eating all portions of the fish remains. With the growing world need for protein, it seems likely that this obstacle will fall and that the lower cost resulting from use of whole fish will make the oceans a much more important factor in the future food supply.

Food by Chemical Processes

The entire farming operation is an anachronism in these times of extensive and advanced production technology. Today we would not consider taking the amount of time in chemical plants that the farmer requires for growing a crop. In an ammonia plant, for example, an operator with two or three helpers can produce 500 to 1000 tons of ammonia in a single day; in contrast, the farmer (also with two or three helpers) requires a whole year to produce about 900 tons of corn.

Much of this low production rate is due to the chemical

complexity of the farmer's product. We can make the simpler chemicals such as ammonia, phosphoric acid, ammonium nitrate, urea, and ammonium phosphate at high rates, but we do not know how to get rapid production of materials such as fats, carbohydrates, and proteins. The molecules are too complicated. We know how to make them but not how to make them rapidly and economically. Someday, perhaps, we will have learned enough to conquer the problem of production economics, but not now.

Currently, and probably for some time to come, we must depend on nature to supply and operate the processes that make our food. About all man can do is set up the "factory" as well as possible, supplying some of the raw materials and keeping adverse growth conditions away from the plant, and then turn the factory over to nature to operate. The operation is slow as are most natural processes; nature is deliberate and it does man no good to get in a hurry. So we plant seeds and wait a season for them to grow and mature; then we feed the crop product to animals and wait another season for them to produce the meat that was the original objective. A more inefficient system is hard to imagine.

Although chemical synthesis of food is not yet on the horizon, some steps have been made in that direction by bringing the farming operation indoors. Yeasts and other microorganisms can be grown at high production rate and the products are good foods.

We should stop here, however, and point out that there is nothing new about bringing farming indoors. Sand or water cultures of plants, with nutrients supplied in the water, have been used successfully for some years. The difficulty again is that nature takes a long time to absorb carbon dioxide from the atmosphere and grow plant substance. For this reason, hydroponics (indoor farming without soil) has not gained much headway.

To get around this problem, chemists have looked for cheap materials to supply carbon dioxide so that they would not have to depend on the atmosphere. They have found what they sought; today chemists in the laboratories of the major oil companies over the world are busily trying to use refined hydrocarbons as the medium for growing yeasts and other microorganisms high in protein. The process is simple; yeast strains (or bacteria), nutrient solution, and hydrocarbon are fed into a fermenter where conditions are carefully controlled to give maximum growth of yeast. The hydrocarbon supplies the carbon, water supplies hydrogen and oxygen, and the nutrient fertilizer solution gives the other elements needed to complete the nutrition of the yeast or bacteria. No contact with the atmosphere is needed, nor is there any need for energy from the sun. The slow pace of photosynthesis is bypassed.

The first commercial protein-from-oil plant was announced in November 1967. The British Petroleum Company is to build a $5,500,000 plant in France, to be completed in 1970 and capable of making over 16,000 tons of protein per year. About 100 tons of oil gives 10 tons of protein concentrate and 90 tons of higher quality oil (since the yeast feeds mainly on the unwanted portions of the oil).

The Russians are also said to have a plant, although few details are available. Engelardt, the distinguished Russian biochemist, is said to have tasted the product and said it is "not as good as roast turkey but may be suitable for sausage."

All this pertains to protein, and to another kind of farming rather than to a true chemical synthesis. Since the yeast and bacteria grow by natural processes, the plant operator is just another type of farmer—growing yeast or bacteria rather than corn or cattle.

But compounds that can supply energy to people, as

fats and carbohydrates do, can also be made from petroleum and by purely chemical processes. Examples are 1,3-butanediol and 2,4-dimethyl heptanoic acid, which supply even more energy per pound than carbohydrates and are suitable for human use.

These are the first halting steps in what may someday be a major food-producing technology—without need for soil, which by then may be taken over anyway for other purposes. The chemists will have solved the mysteries of photosynthesis and giant factories will produce food just as they make the many other needs of man. We can see the mirror image of this, but more advanced, in the textile industry of today. Once cotton, wool, and silk were unchallenged as fibers, and they were grown like food crops—consuming large amounts of labor in the growing and processing. Today the synthetic fibers, nylon, acrilan, orlon, and a host of others, are made from petroleum raw materials in large factories without any need for farm-produced materials.

What will be the place of fertilizers in the food factories of the future? Perhaps a lesser place than today but more likely an even greater one. The proteins will need nitrogen, the processes may need catalysts, and phosphates must be incorporated somewhere to serve the needs of human nutrition. In other words, raw materials and intermediate materials will be needed beyond the basic carbon, hydrogen, and oxygen, just as the farmer needs them today in his management of the natural processes of growth. It is the place of the fertilizer industry, now and in the future, to mine, manufacture, and supply these materials. And since fertilizer producers will be in the forefront of the new technology, perhaps in the future we will have not just a fertilizer industry but a fertilizer-food industry, carrying out in large plants the entire operation of producing food for the teeming billions of tomorrow.

INDEX